OWN YOUR KITCHEN

OWN YOUR
☆ KITCHEN ☆

recipes to inspire & empower

ANNE BURRELL

WITH SUZANNE LENZER

PHOTOGRAPHS BY QUENTIN BACON

Library of Congress Cataloging-in-Publication Data
Burrell, Anne.
  Own your kitchen / Anne Burrell with Suzanne
Lenzer ; photographs by Quentin Bacon.
     pages cm
  Includes index.
  1. Cooking. I. Lenzer, Suzanne. II. Title.

 TX714.B8677 2013
 641.5--dc23

                    2012050250

ISBN 978-0-307-88676-7
eISBN 978-0-385-34557-6

Printed in Hong Kong

Jacket photography by Quentin Bacon

10 9 8 7 6 5 4 3 2 1

First Edition

For Karen—for who you are
and everything you do

CONTENTS

ACKNOWLEDGMENTS

A BIG FAT thank you to all the people in my life who have not only made this book possible, but who are always there with kind words, smiles, love, and support.

My mom, Marlene—my biggest fan and the one who's always there with lots of love and laughter.

My sister Jane—for not only being a great sister but a better friend, and for always having a smile on her face.

The rest of my family—**Ben, Sarah, Jim, Maria, Isabella, Mimi, Nico, Luke, Simon,** and **Maya** for being delightfully fun and nutty and for always asking me, "What's for dinner?"

Christina Cain—a very special friend: I'm very lucky to have a person like you in my life.

Scott Feldman—my manager and friend who handles the business and so much more—thanks for putting up with my crazy!

Sarah Jane Coolahan—my friend and the keeper of my schedule, my sanity, and the person who generally just keeps things together.

Suzanne Lenzer—my wonderful book writer, the one who captures my voice and energy and who gently keeps me on track—thank you!

Quentin Bacon—the wonderfully talented and delightful photographer, with the best name ever, who brought these images to life!

Pat LaFrieda and **Mark Pastore**—my "BIG MEAT" men.

Vivian Lui, Marina Malchin, and **Kristin Walther**—the wonderfully organized, delightfully fun, and quirky team that made the photos in this book so beautiful.

Emily Takoudes and everyone at **Clarkson Potter**—for believing in me and allowing me to put my experiences and recipes on paper.

Jane Treuhaft, Jim Massey, and the entire art and design team—for your direction, colorful creativity, and patience.

Sheri Terry—for making me look pretty and for your "mad yelping" skills.

Janis Donnaud—my book agent. Big fat thanks.

Food Network—for everyone there who has believed in me and allowed me to be my nutty self.

The Key Group—**Jaret Keller, Tara Halper,** and **Rachel Lansing**: Thank you for getting the word out!!!

For my friends—I am a VERY lucky girl to have such an amazing group of people around me who give me their love and support and of course their opinions . . . and who keep me grounded. **Mario Batali, Reyna Mastrosimone, Phil Casaceli, Claire Robinson, Juliet Dannible, Roberto Trevino, Alex Guarnaschelli, Matt Berkowitz,** and **Nick Thorogood,** and **Katie Carey.**

introduction

My life has changed A LOT in the past few years. I've gone from working insane hours in restaurant kitchens to working insane hours in television studios, rushing in and out of airports, and sometimes feeling like I live out of a suitcase. There are times when I just long for the days when I was chained to a restaurant stove! My life is super exciting these days, but there are so many times when I just wish I could stay home, cook dinner, and sit down at my own dining room table to eat it. Because as thankful as I am for all that's happened to me, one thing has not changed: I still love to cook and I love to teach people *how to cook*. Now I just get to do it on a much broader spectrum . . . and I'm extremely lucky.

When I ride my bike around New York City these days, sometimes people wave, they yell, "Hi, Chef Anne!" and they stop me at red lights to share how I helped teach them how to make the perfect roast chicken or they yell, "BTB, RTS!" It always makes me smile and laugh out loud! It's what being on TV has done for me—empowered me to empower home cooks like you. But TV is just the medium to getting the message out there—at the end of the day I'm just a cook. It doesn't matter how many shows I have or how many books I write, cooking is in my soul and if the shows and all the celebrity stuff disappeared tomorrow, I'd go right back into the kitchen and pick up my wooden spoon and start cooking. It's just who I am.

LET'S ROCK YOUR KITCHEN!

Cooking is not rocket science—becoming a good cook is about learning the basics and then applying them. Once you have these principles down you can branch out to different types of cuisines and flavors and get more creative. It's all about understanding the techniques and feeling confident in those skills, trusting yourself and your sense of taste, and deciding where you want to go with it . . . it's up to you! My job is to empower you to become the best cook you can be and to learn to own your kitchen. Why? Because cooking is fun—and delicious.

I feel very grateful to spend my life doing something I love SOOOOO much. Certainly I loved working in restaurants, and like most chefs, I focused on one type of cuisine and worked hard to do it really well. As I've progressed in my career, I've branched out beyond my rustic Italian roots. I love that people don't watch my show to learn how to cook rustic Italian food; they watch my show to *learn how to cook.*

My mother often asks me where I come up with ideas for my recipes. I always say the same thing: I don't know! Every time I have to sit down and write new recipes I'm totally stuck at first. Then I start to think about what I've tasted lately that's turned me on—I may be really into ramen at that moment, craving spicy curries, or excited by Spanish flavors. Cooking is an incredible way to experience the world and to bring amazing flavors out there into your own home. To me, food is the only truly universal language (every living thing has to eat!) and you can learn a ton about people and other cultures through their food.

My recipes pull from all my many experiences—they are influenced by the people, places, and tastes that inspire me and are brought together in a way that I think will be delicious. It doesn't matter where the inspiration comes from—it only matters that you're open to new experiences and that you have the skills to help you accomplish whatever it is *you* want to cook. And then COOK IT LIKE YOU OWN IT!

a girl chef on the go

Since I left the daily life of a restaurant chef, everything has changed. I used to know that Tuesday through Saturday I'd be at the restaurant for twelve hours a day cooking, dealing with deliveries, staff, customers, and even broken toilets—but at least I knew it would all happen in the same building. Today I never know exactly where I'll be or what I'll be doing! My family and friends text me and say, "Where in the world is Anne Burrell?" I'm not complaining; I love my life! I love the adventure of it and the not knowing what's next. But it's SOOOOO different than it was just a few years ago.

A great part of this new routine is that I have met SO many amazing people and eat lots of delicious food. Wherever I go, I always try to build in a little time for myself to discover something new, and I've found that every city or town has something special to offer. I love the Westside Market in Cleveland and the Rock and Roll Hall of Fame, when I was in Dallas I picked at a business lunch and then headed straight to a BBQ joint recommended by the locals, and in Hawaii I got up at five in the morning to see the tuna market in action. But even when I'm in New York City, I treasure every opportunity thrown my way and each one ultimately influences me when I'm developing new recipes. So many times when I'm having all these experiences, I just sit back and say: Wow! Going to culinary school got me here???

excuse me while i dive into something more comfortable!

I don't get to cook for myself and my friends as often as I used to. So when I am home, I don't want to go out for a fancy dinner and I certainly don't want another club sandwich from room service!!! I just want to put on my stretchy pants, drink a glass (or two!) of wine, and eat good old homemade food and catch up with my friends. I can't

wait to dive into a great dish of pasta, whip up a fabulous chopped salad with warm goat cheese, or dig into a great turkey burger. And that's what this book is about.

I see the world through food, and these are my interpretations of my experiences and the recipes that I have incorporated into my home life. This collection includes many of my new favorites, the ones I make for myself and for my friends and family when we're just hanging out. My food isn't fussy (that doesn't mean I don't pay attention to detail!): I always have good *mise en place,* I always clean as I go, and I'm always doing QC (quality control) and making sure things taste delicious. But the food itself is homey and comfy. You'll find a great brined turkey for your Thanksgiving feast, some seriously killer sandwiches, and amazing brunches among other yummy dishes. It's a collection of recipes that I've put together because I LOOOOOVE them—and that's the beautiful thing about cooking, there's always room for new recipes in your arsenal.

This book is meant to build your confidence in the kitchen, and to make cooking approachable and fun. My goal is to get you to be excited about making dinner, to start thinking like a chef, to try new things and experience new flavors—and then TO OWN IT!!! So grab these recipes, cook them, and kill them with deliciousness!

10 WAYS TO OWN YOUR KITCHEN

I know I've said all this before but I have to say it again because these are basic culinary principles that I'm super passionate about—and if you stick to them (like you should!) they will help you become a rock star at the stove.

1 **Read a recipe all the way through,** *before* **you start cooking.** This is the step that nobody ever wants to do and it's the one that will help prevent mistakes. By reading the recipe first you know where you're heading in a recipe—from the prep work to cooking time—and exactly what you need in terms of ingredients and equipment.

2 **Do your** *mise en place. Mise en place* translates to "put in place" and it means to get all of your prep work done before you start cooking. By getting all your ingredients ready and your equipment out before you get to the stove, you'll be an organized cook and you can clean as you go. And you won't get stuck trying to come up with creative solutions for problems or being bunched up because you're working in the middle of clutter. Good *mise en place* will make cooking less stressful for you, more fun, and delicious. It's a win-win-win!

3 **Taste and season as you go.** Many home cooks practice the "I-hope-it-comes-out-all-right" method of cooking—they don't taste their food during the cooking process and then wonder why it isn't delicious when it's done. As a cook, you must taste your food and season it throughout the cooking process. FOOD SHOULD TASTE GOOD! If you don't taste it throughout the cooking process there's no way for you to know what it tastes like or to fix it if something is wrong. Your palate is just like any other muscle and you need to learn to train it. The only way to do this is to taste your food!!!

4 **Embrace salt.** Salt is a flavor enhancer and it brings out the natural flavors in food. IT MAKES THINGS TASTE *MORE*. If you don't cook with salt you will never be a good cook . . . there, I said it. Accept it and move on. If you cook from scratch using fresh ingredients (meaning seasonal produce and high-quality meat) you can salt with reckless abandon and you'll never get close to anything that has been processed or packaged. Cook from scratch and season with salt.

5 **Salt and pepper are not married, they're only dating.** Salt and pepper do not serve the same function so they don't need to be used together. I'm not a gratuitous pepper girl—I use pepper as an ingredient, it's a spice that adds another strong flavor. It does not

have the same function as salt. For some reason people tend to be freaked out about too much salt but they go hog wild with pepper. Pepper adds an entirely different flavor to food. I would never think of adding salt and *horseradish* to everything! It's the same with pepper.

6 **Fresh herbs rock, dried herbs don't.** I'd rather cook without herbs than use dried herbs, which are nothing like their fresh counterparts. In my opinion, most dried herbs don't taste very good. Adding something that doesn't taste good to your dish usually doesn't make it taste better. So here's my professional advice: Don't do it.

7 **Spices are sexy!** Spices add taste, aroma, and warmth to food. They're seeds, bark, and pods that can transform a dish from good to great—but they need to be treated with respect. Buy them in small amounts and replace them annually. It's also best to buy them in their whole form and toast them in a dry sauté pan for 3 or 4 minutes until they're super aromatic. Then grind them in a spice grinder (a coffee grinder used just for spices).

8 **Toast your nuts—it makes them browner and crunchier, and brings out their full nutty flavor.** To make sure nuts toast evenly, put them on a baking sheet in a 350°F. oven. How long does it take for nuts to toast? Just long enough to forget! Start with about 6 to 7 minutes, but keep any eye on them and set a timer. Once you start to smell them it's too late!

9 **The right equipment makes cooking fun.** Having the tools you need to cook the dishes you want is important, but you don't have to run out and buy everything all at once. Add the ones that excite you to your birthday list! Start by getting yourself set up with some basics: pots and pans, bowls, wooden spoons, spatulas, measuring cups and spoons, and then add as you need to. Once you start cooking you'll gradually collect more stuff and then you'll want even more—kitchen tools are addictive!

10 **Keep your pantry stocked.** I'm all about fresh produce and meat, but a well-stocked pantry will make cooking easier and more enjoyable. Start with some basics—good quality olive oil, kosher salt, Parmigiano, garlic, dried pasta, canned tomatoes and beans, bread crumbs, spices, and so on—and keep adding to it as you go along. With a package of pasta in the house and a few other staples you'll always be able to whip up a delicious meal!

firsts

wilted romaine salad
with roasted pears, taleggio,
and hazelnuts   21

tomato salad
with shrimp and black
volcanic sea salt   22

insalata "chopata"
with warm goat cheese   25

kale caesar salad   26

bacon-wrapped dates
with chorizo and manchego   29

ahi poke
with macadamia nuts   30

shrimp
in garlic olive oil and chilies   33

marinated white anchovies
with cucumbers, ruby red grapefruit,
and cilantro   34

steamed clams
with tomato and fennel   37

scotch eggs   38

tortilla española
with garlic aïoli   40

mushroom soup
with bacon   42

cauliflower "steaks"
with sautéed porcini and
a poached egg   43

zucchini cannelloni
with fresh tomato sauce   46

ricotta flan
with bacon, corn, cherry tomatoes,
and arugula pesto   49

pork and potato
empanadas
with charred tomatillo sauce   52

bacalao fritters
with piquillo pepper and marcona
almond sauce   56

homemade pita bread
with pickled feta spread   59

I've said it before and I'll say it again:

I LOOOOOVE appetizers. When I was studying in Italy I was introduced to the world of antipasti—also called firsts, starters, or simply apps—and it totally changed the way I like to eat. There's something so tantalizing about smaller bites, the excitement of getting to enjoy a variety of flavors when you're really hungry at the beginning of a meal, when your palate is most sensitive and can really discern all the different tastes and textures going on.

I also ADORE appetizers because I find they're almost always more creative than main dishes. For some reason chefs don't feel like they have to follow the rules when it comes to apps—they're freer and more playful with combinations. And breaking the rules can be liberating and empowering—it opens up an entire world of possibilities in the kitchen! The same cooking techniques apply, of course—a sauté is still a sauté and a braise is still a braise—BUT there's no compulsion to put a protein, a starch, and a veg together. You can do anything. YOU CAN EVEN MAKE A WHOLE MEAL OUT OF JUST STARTERS!

A starter can be a cold soup or a warm salad, a savory tart or a sweet crostini, even a trio of creamy croquettes. A great starter can be smoky, spicy, sweet, salty, or a combo—it can blend different flavor profiles and different ingredients that all work together to create something delicious. The recipes in this chapter are exactly that: A collection of dishes that I love to eat anywhere, anytime. They're interpretations inspired by my journey—starting from my roots in rustic Italian food and moving beyond to incorporate other flavors and ingredients that keep me excited and energized at the stove.

Don't get hung up thinking first courses have to be a specific way—remember, you're the chef of your own kitchen! A great starter can be ANYTHING—whatever you want—just make it delicious, and, of course, small! And you know what happens when you shrink something? It just gets cuter!!!

wilted romaine salad
with roasted pears, taleggio, and hazelnuts

SERVES 4 TIME **ABOUT 40 MINUTES**

I'm a huge fan of wilted salads. I'm the girl who dresses her salad and eats it an hour later. And I'm always up for topping a salad with hot stuff. But, I also love a bit of crunch mixed up with something warm and wilted. That's why I created this salad: The warmish romaine is lovely with a nice soft, super-ripe, juicy pear, some melted stinky cheese, and the exciting crunch of toasted hazelnuts. It's got a bit of everything going on all at once. It's one sexy salad.

MISE EN PLACE

2 Bosc pears, peeled, halved, and cored

Extra virgin olive oil

1/2 pound ripe Taleggio cheese, outer rind removed

2 hearts of romaine, each quartered lengthwise, stalk left intact

Kosher salt

1/2 small red onion, cut into rings

1/4 cup champagne vinegar

1 teaspoon Dijon mustard

Big fat finishing oil

1/4 cup hazelnuts, toasted and coarsely chopped

1 Preheat the oven to 350°F.

2 Place the pears on a baking sheet and toss with olive oil. Roast for 15 minutes, turn the pears, and cook for another 15 minutes. Remove from the oven and reserve.

3 Place the Taleggio in the microwave for 1 minute or in the oven for about 5 minutes. You want the Taleggio soft and very pungent (SO YUM!!!).

4 Heat a grill pan or a grill lined with foil. In a large bowl, toss the romaine wedges with olive oil and salt. Grill the romaine and the onions for 1 to 2 minutes on each side, or until they are slightly charred and wilty.

5 Place 2 romaine wedges on each plate; scatter the onions on top. Keeping the stem end of each pear half intact, cut the pears in half. Lean the pretty, pretty pears on the romaine wedges. Drizzle the melted cheese over the pears and romaine and let it set up.

6 In a small dish or measuring cup, combine the vinegar, mustard, and a couple tablespoons of big fat finishing oil. Taste and season with salt if needed. Drizzle the vinaigrette over each salad and sprinkle with the hazelnuts.

serve this and there will be nothing romaine-ing - it's THAT good!

tomato salad

with shrimp and black volcanic sea salt

SERVES **4 TO 6**   TIME **ABOUT 20 MINUTES**

When I was in Hawaii I had this version of a tomato salad with shrimp and volcanic salt, and it was amazing. First of all, it looks beautiful—the red tomatoes, pink shrimp, and inky black crystals on top are a vision of delightfulness. Then you take that first bite and the little salt crystals give up their crunchy, oceanic, mineral-y salinity. Next you taste the sweet shrimp, like they jumped right out of the water and onto your plate. And of course fresh, sweet, juicy, slightly acidic tomatoes bring it all together. It's not just another tomato salad—it's a party in your mouth!

MISE EN PLACE

Extra virgin olive oil

4 cloves garlic, smashed

Crushed red pepper

1 pound large shrimp, peeled and deveined

Kosher salt

$\frac{1}{2}$ pint heirloom cherry tomatoes, halved

1 pound heirloom tomatoes, cut in various shapes

$\frac{1}{2}$ white onion (if you have a Maui onion, that's great), thinly sliced

6 large fresh basil leaves, cut into a chiffonade

$\frac{1}{4}$ cup red wine vinegar

Black volcanic sea salt

ANNE-NOTATION Okay, so you may not have a volcano in your backyard or access to volcanic salt at your grocery store. But you can get it online or use another kind of big, flaky salt like Maldon—it's really just about feeling that salty punctuation in contrast to the sweet tomatoes and shrimp.

1   Coat a large sauté pan with olive oil. Add the garlic and a pinch of crushed red pepper and bring the pan to high heat. When the garlic is golden and very aromatic, about 2 minutes, remove it and ditch it—it has fulfilled its garlic destiny. Toss in the shrimp, season with kosher salt, and cook for 2 to 3 minutes, or until the shrimp turn pink on the outside and are opaque all the way through. Remove from the heat and reserve.

2   In a large bowl, combine all the tomatoes, onion, basil, and a pinch of crushed red pepper. Add the vinegar and the juices from the pan. Toss gently.

3   Arrange the salad on serving plates and top with the shrimp. Sprinkle with the sea salt and serve.

you say tomato ... I say "SUPER YUM"!!

insalata "chopata"

with warm goat cheese

SERVES 4 TIME ABOUT 30 MINUTES

When I worked at Felidia in New York City, the ladies who lunch would come in and order a salad. I can't tell you how many times a day the waiters would bring the salads back to the kitchen and say, "Can you chop this please? She'd like it chopped." So the waiters started calling this salad "chopata," because in Italian when you add "ata" to a word it puts it in the past tense. It's a yummy salad made of crispy, crunchy lettuce, fennel, carrots, and chickpeas, but really anything goes here.

MISE EN PLACE

2 large eggs

1 cup carrots, peeled and cut into 1/4-inch dice

1/2 small red onion, cut into 1/4-inch dice

1 cup fennel, cut into 1/4-inch dice

1 cup celery, peeled and cut into 1/4-inch dice

1 cup canned chickpeas, drained and rinsed

1 romaine heart (or 1/2 head iceberg), cut into a chiffonade

1 cup fresh or canned corn kernels

1 cup cucumber, peeled, seeded, and cut into 1/4-inch dice

1/4 cup salted sunflower seeds

1/2 bunch of fresh oregano, leaves finely chopped

3 tablespoons big fat finishing oil

1/3 cup red wine vinegar

Kosher salt

6 ounces goat cheese

1 Put the eggs in a small saucepan, add water to cover by an inch, and bring to a boil over high heat. COVER THE PAN!!! Remove from the heat and set the timer. Leave the eggs in the covered pot for 13 minutes . . . eggs-actly! Remove the eggs from the hot water and let cool.

2 In a large bowl, combine the carrots, onion, fennel, celery, chickpeas, romaine, corn, cucumber, sunflower seeds, and oregano. Toss to combine.

3 Peel and chop the eggs and toss them in with the veggies.

4 In a measuring cup, combine the oil and vinegar. Whisk to combine and add to the veggies. Season with salt and taste.

5 Place the goat cheese in a heatproof dish and warm in a microwave for 1 1/2 minutes or in a 300°F oven for 10 minutes.

6 Stir the salad, taste, and reseason if needed. Divide the salad among 4 serving plates and top each with a dollop of the warm goat cheese to serve.

chop- chop !!!

kale caesar salad

SERVES 2 TO 4   TIME ABOUT 20 MINUTES

Everywhere I go these days I hear "kale, kale, kale!" It's the new superfood, so I thought I'd join the bandwagon—but with a twist. Often with raw kale salads there's a lot of chewing involved, which isn't that delightful, so I decided to treat the kale more delicately. I cut out the rib and slice the leaves thinly so they're almost dainty. Drizzle these lovely green ribbons with some super-acidic dressing and this salad doesn't taste like it's good for you—it just tastes good! You'll want to hoover this salad down all day long!

MISE EN PLACE

Extra virgin olive oil

4 cloves garlic, smashed

Pinch of crushed
   red pepper

2 slices of day-old Italian
   bread, cut into ½-inch
   cubes

½ cup grated Parmigiano

Zest and juice of 1 lemon

1 tablespoon Dijon mustard

2 to 3 anchovy fillets

2 shakes Worcestershire
   sauce

Kosher salt

1 bunch of kale, tough
   stems removed, cut into
   ribbons

1   Coat a large sauté pan with olive oil. Toss in half the garlic and the crushed red pepper and bring the pan to medium heat. Cook the garlic until it becomes golden and very aromatic, 2 to 3 minutes. Remove the garlic and ditch it—it has fulfilled its garlic destiny. Toss in the bread cubes and cook, stirring frequently, until they are golden, crisp, and have absorbed all the oil, like little olive oil sponges. Remove from the heat and reserve.

2   In the bowl of a food processor, combine the Parmigiano, lemon zest and juice, the remaining garlic, the Dijon, anchovies, and Worcestershire.

Purée until the mixture is smooth, 15 to 20 seconds. With the machine running, add ¼ to ⅓ cup olive oil through the feed tube. Let the processor continue to run for another 10 to 15 seconds. Taste and season with salt if needed.

3   In a large bowl, toss the kale with the croutons and two-thirds of the dressing. Let the kale sit for 3 to 4 minutes to soften. Taste, add the remaining dressing, and adjust the seasoning if needed.

hail to the caesar ... salad !!

bacon-wrapped dates
with chorizo and manchego

MAKES **12 PIECES** TIME **ABOUT 20 MINUTES**

I first had bacon-wrapped dates in Spain and I was like, you know what would make these better? CHORIZO! I love the idea of a bacon-wrapped date, but I love the idea of bacon-wrapped dates with chorizo and Manchego even more! Make these ahead of time if you're having a cocktail party, and then just warm them in the oven—or plunk them on a salad for a fabulous starter. Brush the dates with a bit of maple syrup and some sherry vinegar and these are a sweet, sticky, sour treat that will definitely make you feel like a rock star host.

MISE EN PLACE

12 Medjool dates, pitted

1/2 pound Manchego cheese, cut into 12 rectangular logs

3 links fresh chorizo, casings removed

6 slices of bacon, cut in half

1/4 cup maple syrup

2 tablespoons sherry vinegar

1   Preheat the oven to 375°F.

2   Make an incision lengthwise in each date, open it up, and flatten.

3   Place a piece of Manchego in the center of each date.

4   Break each chorizo link into quarters. Form each piece of chorizo into a log the length of the date and squish it onto the Manchego. Close the date around the filling and squeeze to secure. Wrap each date with a piece of bacon and secure with a toothpick.

5   Place all the dates on a baking sheet, transfer to the oven, and roast for 7 to 8 minutes, or until the bacon is starting to crisp up. Turn the dates over and roast for another 7 to 8 minutes.

6   In a small bowl, combine the syrup and vinegar.

7   Remove the dates from the oven and brush them with the syrup-vinegar mixture. Return the dates to the oven and bake for another 1 to 2 minutes, or until they are crackly and sticky. Remove from the oven and let rest for a minute, remove the toothpicks, and serve.

It's a date!

ahi poke
with macadamia nuts

SERVES 2 TO 4 TIME ABOUT 40 MINUTES

I thought I really didn't need another tuna tartare in my life—tartare schmartar. BTDT (been there, done that!). Then I had poke at this divey place in Waikiki that my friend Vikram Garg, who's also a chef, took me to. I can't remember the name of the place, but man do I remember the poke! I hoovered the whole dish . . . the freshest tuna perfectly dressed in soy sauce and rice wine vinegar with a crunch of fresh macadamia nuts right out of the shell—they were SOOOOO crunchy and delicious. It was a night I will always remember—a place where you can eat poke like that, have a few drinks, and then get up and do karaoke.

MISE EN PLACE

- 1 clove garlic, smashed and very finely chopped
- 1-inch piece of fresh ginger, peeled and grated
- ½ cup soy sauce, plus a little more if desired
- ¼ cup rice wine vinegar
- 1 teaspoon toasted sesame oil
- 2 teaspoons sambal oelek or Asian chili paste
- 1 pound Ahi tuna, cut into ½-inch dice
- 1 small onion, Maui if available, julienned
- 3 scallions, whites sliced very thin on a severe bias, greens sliced and reserved
- 3 tablespoons toasted and coarsely chopped macadamia nuts

1 In a small bowl, combine the garlic, ginger, soy sauce, vinegar, sesame oil, and sambal.

2 In a medium bowl, combine the tuna, onion, and scallion whites. Add the soy mixture and stir well to combine. Cover and refrigerate for 30 minutes.

3 Remove the tuna from the fridge and let sit at room temperature for 5 minutes. Taste and season with more soy if needed. Toss in the macadamia nuts and garnish with the scallion greens. Serve immediately.

poked right from the ocean!

shrimp
in garlic olive oil and chilies

SERVES 4 TIME ABOUT 15 MINUTES

This is one of those super-simple dishes with only a few ingredients, but incredibly complex flavor. The key here is infusing the olive oil with the garlic and chilies and then cooking the shrimp tenderly, quickly, and with respect. You warm up the oil with the aromatics and then, when it's piping hot, add the shrimp and pull the pan off the heat so the shrimp cook gently and stay succulent. It's really that simple—the only other thing you need is a whole lot of bread for dunking (a bottle of wine doesn't hurt either).

MISE EN PLACE

Extra virgin olive oil

11 cloves garlic, 10 smashed plus 1 whole clove

4 dried chilies, broken into pieces

4 thick slices of rustic Italian bread

1 pound small shrimp (21–25 are great), peeled and deveined

Kosher salt

Juice of 1 lemon

1 bunch of fresh Italian parsley, leaves finely chopped

2 cups baby arugula

ANNE-NOTATION The point here is to cook the shrimp really quickly in super-hot olive oil, so it's best to work in batches.

1   Generously coat a large sauté pan with olive oil and toss in 5 of the smashed garlic cloves and 2 of the broken chilies. Bring the pan to high heat—it should be screaming hot!

2   Toast or grill the bread, then rub each slice with the whole garlic clove, drizzle with olive oil, and keep in a warm spot.

3   As the garlic starts to just SLIGHTLY turn brown, toss in half the shrimp and season with salt. Stir and cook for 1 minute or until the shrimp just turn pink. Remove from the heat, and immediately stir in half the lemon juice and half the parsley. Transfer the shrimp to a dish and keep warm. Repeat this entire process with the remaining ingredients.

4   Divide the arugula among 4 serving bowls, top with shrimp, and drizzle with the cooking juices. Cut each slice of toast in half on the bias and tuck the bread into the side of the bowl. Serve immediately.

shrimp - alicious !

marinated white anchovies

with cucumbers, ruby red grapefruit, and cilantro

SERVES 4 TO 6 TIME ABOUT 20 MINUTES

Once upon a time I found myself on a true rock star vacation. I was with Mario Batali and Michael Stipe in Portofino, Italy, and we were invited to join one of their friends on his yacht. We went snorkeling and the sun was shining through the crystal-clear blue waters, and there was this enormous Jesus statue at the bottom of the ocean being swarmed by a million silver anchovies—literally a wall of silver. So now, whenever I think of marinated anchovies, I think of this incredible experience.

MISE EN PLACE

½ English cucumber, cut on the bias into ¼-inch slices, then julienned

1 Ruby Red grapefruit, supremed, each section cut into thirds and juice reserved

1 small red onion, very thinly sliced

1 bunch of fresh cilantro, leaves removed, stems chopped

2 tablespoons champagne vinegar

Big fat finishing oil

Kosher salt

Pinch of crushed red pepper

20 to 24 marinated white anchovy fillets

ANNE-NOTATION Be sure to supreme (see page 252) the grapefruit over a bowl so you catch the juice—then squeeze the membranes to extract ALL the juice. You want all this goodness to dress the salad.

1 In a medium bowl, combine the cucumber, grapefruit, and red onion. Toss together and reserve.

2 In a food processor, combine the cilantro stems, grapefruit juice, and vinegar. With the machine running, slowly drizzle in 2 tablespoons big fat finishing oil. Season with salt and crushed red pepper, and taste to make sure it is delicious.

3 Toss the cucumber mixture with half the vinaigrette.

4 Divide the anchovies among 4 to 6 serving plates, laying them side by side in the middle of each plate.

5 Add the cilantro leaves to the cuke mixture and place a quarter of the salad on each plate, arranging it in a line on top of the anchovies. Spoon a bit more vinaigrette over each plate and serve immediately.

go fish!

steamed clams
with tomato and fennel

SERVES 4 TIME ABOUT 30 MINUTES

I love clams, I love clams, I love clams! The salty, briny, oceanic flavor of clams is one of the best things around. Make this dish for a starter and serve a handful to each guest, or ratchet it up and make a whole pot for an entrée. Just be sure to sop up all the super-flavorful yummy juices when you're done!

MISE EN PLACE

Extra virgin olive oil

5 cloves garlic, 4 very thinly sliced plus 1 whole clove

1/2 fennel bulb, tough core removed, thinly sliced

Kosher salt

Pinch of crushed red pepper

2 beefsteak tomatoes, cored, seeded, and cut into 1/4-inch dice

2 dozen littleneck clams, scrubbed

2 cups dry white wine

4 thick slices rustic Italian bread

1 teaspoon fennel pollen or fennel seeds, toasted and ground

1 bunch of fresh chives, finely chopped

1 Coat a large pot with olive oil and bring it to medium heat. When the oil is hot, add the sliced garlic and fennel, and season with salt and crushed red pepper. Cook until the fennel begins to soften, 5 to 6 minutes. Add the tomatoes to the pan and cook for another 3 to 4 minutes.

2 Crank up the heat to high. When the pan is very hot and the tomato mixture bubbling, toss in the clams and stir to combine.

3 Cook the clams for 2 to 3 minutes, then add the white wine. Cover and cook until the clams open, 5 to 7 minutes. Remove the open clams and set aside. Continue to cook any unopened clams for another couple of minutes; if they still don't open, discard them.

4 While the clams are steaming, toast or grill the bread. Rub the bread with the whole garlic clove and drizzle generously with olive oil. Keep in a warm spot.

5 Transfer the clams to serving dishes and pour the tomato mixture and fennel and all the yummy juices over the clams. Give each dish a sprinkle of fennel pollen and chives. Serve immediately with the toasts.

i'm happy as a vongole! (that's clam in Italian) :)

scotch eggs

SERVES 2 TO 4 TIME ABOUT 1 HOUR

Here we are, back in one of my favorite places—eggland! I first had these soft-boiled eggs wrapped in sausage, then breaded and deep-fried, in England and they were enough to make me not want to leave the UK.

MISE EN PLACE

4 large eggs

1 pound bulk sausage

1/2 bunch of fresh sage, leaves finely chopped

1/2 teaspoon crushed red pepper (optional)

1 cup all-purpose flour

2 large eggs beaten with 2 tablespoons water

2 cups panko bread crumbs

2 quarts peanut or other neutral-flavored oil

Kosher salt

ANNE ALERT It's best to soft-boil the eggs ahead of time, so plan accordingly.

1 Place 4 eggs in a small saucepan with water to cover by an inch. Bring the water to a boil (BTB), COVER, TURN OFF THE HEAT, and let sit for 5 minutes—EGGS-ACTLY. Remove the eggs from the pan and transfer to an ice bath.

2 Keeping the eggs submerged in the cold water while you work, carefully peel the eggs. The yolks will still be a bit runny, so be careful not to break the whites.

3 In a medium bowl, combine the sausage, sage, and crushed red pepper, if using, along with 2 to 3 tablespoons water. Knead the mixture to get the sausage really pliable and to combine everything really well.

4 Coat each egg with a quarter of the sausage mixture, transfer the eggs to a dish, and reserve in the fridge.

5 Set up your standard breading procedure: 1 bowl of flour, 1 bowl with the egg-water mixture, and 1 bowl of bread crumbs. Using one hand for dry things and one hand for wet things, run each egg through the flour, shaking off any excess, then coat it in the egg mixture, then the panko. Place the dredged eggs back in the fridge.

6 In a deep medium saucepan, heat the oil until it reaches 350°F or until it sizzles when you flick in a bit of flour. While the oil heats up, line a baking sheet with paper towels and set it next to the stove. Working in batches, fry the eggs in the oil until they are lovely, crisp, fairly dark brown, about 10 minutes.

7 Using a slotted spoon, remove the eggs from the pan, drain on the paper towels, sprinkle with salt, and serve hot or at room temperature.

great Scott-ish egg !

tortilla española
with garlic aïoli

SERVES **4 TO 8** TIME **ABOUT 1 HOUR**

I've had a lot of versions of this Spanish dish—it's available at every tapas joint in this country and in Spain. The traditional tortilla is made from two of my very favorite foods: eggs and potatoes, and it can be a super-yum, go-to dish for entertaining or a light lunch, especially because you can make it ahead and serve it at room temperature. Ultimately it's a big, thick, delicious egg and potato pie! Make this for brunch or lunch, for snacking tapas-style with a glass of wine, even for dinner with a salad—it's pretty much just a perfect meal no matter how you slice it (I prefer big wedges!).

MISE EN PLACE

FOR THE TORTILLA

2½ pounds Yukon gold potatoes, peeled and cut into ½-inch dice

1 onion, cut into ¼-inch dice

1 cup plus 1 tablespoon extra virgin olive oil

Kosher salt

Pinch of crushed red pepper

8 large eggs, beaten

FOR THE AÏOLI

1 large egg yolk

2 cloves garlic, smashed and finely chopped

2 tablespoons fresh lemon juice

½ cup vegetable or other neutral-flavored oil

Kosher salt

FOR THE TORTILLA

1   In a large bowl, combine the potatoes and onion. Drizzle with about half of the olive oil and season with salt and a pinch of crushed red pepper.

2   Transfer the onion-potato mixture to a 12-inch nonstick sauté pan. Add the remaining olive oil, bring the pan to medium heat, and cook for 30 to 35 minutes, or until the potatoes are tender and cooked through.

3   Using a colander or mesh strainer, strain the oil from the potatoes and onions into a bowl. Add 1 tablespoon of the olive oil from the potatoes to the beaten eggs and reserve the rest. Season the eggs with salt.

4   Return the vegetable mixture to the sauté pan and bring the pan to medium heat. Add the egg mixture, cover the pan, and cook for 10 to 12 minutes, or until the eggs are just set. Remove the pan from the heat, leaving it covered, and let sit for another 10 minutes.

5   Holding the lid on the pan, in one swift movement, flip the pan so the tortilla is sitting on the inside of the lid. Slide the

tortilla back into the pan—the bottom is now the top—and cook for 2 minutes over medium heat to make sure the eggs are fully cooked. Remove the pan from the heat and let the tortilla come to room temperature.

FOR THE AÏOLI

1   In the bowl of a food processor, combine the egg yolk, garlic, and lemon juice and purée.

2   With the machine running, add the oil drop by drop until the mixture is thick and homogeneous. At this point you can add the remaining oil in a SLOW, steady stream.

3   With the machine still running, add ½ cup of the reserved olive oil from cooking the potatoes. Season with salt, then taste and adjust the seasoning if needed. The aïoli should be pourable, but still very thick. If it's too thick, add a couple drops of water. If too thin, add a few more drops of the reserved olive oil while the machine is running.

OLE , OLE , OLE !!!

mushroom soup
with bacon

SERVES 4 TIME ABOUT 1½ HOURS

I'm not much of a cream soup girl, but when I was Ireland for a wedding I had the most delicious bowl of cream of mushroom soup. I ate it to be polite, but after a few spoonfuls, I knew it was something to write home about. I don't usually do the cream and butter routine, so I've tweaked this recipe to lighten it up by thickening it with potatoes and just a shot of cream . . . and of course bacon!

MISE EN PLACE

5 slices bacon, cut into lardons

Extra virgin olive oil

2 pounds mixed mushrooms (shiitake, cremini, and oyster), stemmed and sliced

Kosher salt

1 onion, cut into ¼-inch dice

1 clove garlic, smashed and finely chopped

1 large potato, peeled and cut into 1-inch dice

½ cup dry sherry

1 quart chicken or veggie stock

½ cup heavy cream

½ bunch of fresh Italian parsley, leaves finely chopped

1 Toss the bacon into a large wide pot, add a drizzle of olive oil, and bring the pan to medium heat. Cook the bacon until it's brown and crispy and has given off a lot of fat. Transfer the bacon to paper towels to drain.

2 Crank up the heat to high and add the mushrooms and season with salt and stir. If the mushrooms soak up all of the fat, add a couple more drops of olive oil. Cook the mushrooms until they become soft and release their juices, 5 to 6 minutes. Remove the mushrooms and reserve.

3 Toss the onion into the pot and season with salt. Reduce the heat to medium. Add a few drops of oil if needed. Cook the onion until soft and aromatic, 8 to 10 minutes. Add the garlic and cook until aromatic, 1 to 2 minutes.

4 Return two-thirds of the mushrooms to the pot along with the diced potato.

5 Add the sherry and cook until it has evaporated by half. Add the stock, bring to a boil, reduce to a simmer (BTB, RTS), and cook for 30 minutes. Add the cream and simmer for 10 minutes more.

6 Using a blender or an immersion blender, purée the soup until smooth. Taste to make sure it's delicious.

7 Add the reserved mushrooms and half the bacon. Serve immediately, garnished with the remaining bacon and chopped parsley.

magic mushroom . . . soup!

cauliflower "steaks"
with sautéed porcini and a poached egg

SERVES 4 TIME ABOUT 1 HOUR

This is a winning dish, literally. In the finals of *Worst Cooks in America* against Bobby Flay, this was part of the entrée—which included a steak and roasted kale chips—that led us to victory. During the practice round, when Bobby saw this, he said, "Ah, man, this is gonna put you over the edge!" Then when we won, all the judges kept saying, "We're totally gonna steal this idea!" And they can—but it's mine first, and I want to share it with you. It's a simple but cool and innovative way to cut and roast cauliflower so it has the textural feel of a steak. This dish is so good that my recruit Kelly brought home a lot of money because of it!

MISE EN PLACE

FOR THE CAULIFLOWER

1 head of cauliflower, trimmed and cut into four ¹/₂-inch cross-section slices from the middle, rounded outside edges removed and cut into bite-size florets

Extra virgin olive oil

Kosher salt

FOR THE PORCINI

¹/₂ pound pancetta, cut into ¹/₄-inch dice

Extra virgin olive oil

2 cloves garlic, smashed

1 pound porcini or portobello mushrooms, cleaned and cut into ¹/₂-inch dice

2 sprigs of fresh rosemary, leaves finely chopped

Salt

Pinch of crushed red pepper

¹/₂ cup dry white wine

FOR THE EGGS

3 tablespoons white vinegar

4 large eggs

Salt

1 bunch of fresh chives, finely chopped

FOR THE CAULIFLOWER

1   Preheat the oven to 375°F.

2   On a baking sheet, toss the cauliflower florets with olive oil and salt. Add the "steaks" to the baking sheet, coat with olive oil, and season with salt. Bake for 20 minutes, then flip the steaks and stir the florets. Bake for another 15 to 20 minutes or until the cauliflower is soft and brown. Remove from the oven and reserve.

FOR THE PORCINI

1   Toss the pancetta in a large sauté pan with a few drops of olive oil and bring the pan to medium-low heat. Cook the pancetta, stirring occasionally, until it is brown and crispy and has rendered some fat, 8 to 10 minutes.

★ ★
★

(recipe continues)

2   Toss in the garlic and cook until golden and aromatic, 2 to 3 minutes. Remove the garlic and ditch it—it has fulfilled its garlic destiny.

3   Crank up the heat to medium-high. When the fat starts to sizzle, toss in the mushrooms and rosemary and stir to combine. Season with salt and crushed red pepper. If the pan seems dry, add a few more drops of olive oil. Cook the mushrooms, stirring occasionally, until they start to soften, 3 to 4 minutes.

4   Add the wine. Using a wooden spoon, scrape any brown deliciousness off the bottom of the pan. Continue to cook the mushrooms until most of the wine has evaporated. Remove from the heat, taste, and reseason if needed. Toss in the reserved cauliflower and keep warm over low heat.

my favorite flower!!

TO POACH THE EGGS

1   Fill a medium saucepan two-thirds of the way with water and add the vinegar. Bring the water to a boil (BTB), then reduce the heat until no bubbles break the surface of the water. You are creating a very gentle cooking environment—like an egg Jacuzzi.

2   Break the eggs very close to the surface of the water and cook for 4 minutes or until the whites are cooked through and the yolks are warm and runny.

TO ASSEMBLE

1   Place a cauliflower "steak" on each serving plate and top each with a spoonful of the porcini hash.

2   Using a slotted spoon, carefully remove each egg from the poaching liquid and make a pit stop on a paper towel to blot any excess water. Nestle an egg on top of the porcini and cauliflower. Sprinkle the eggs with a few grains of salt and some chives and serve immediately.

zucchini cannelloni
with fresh tomato sauce

MAKES ABOUT 12 CANNELLONI TIME ABOUT 1½ HOURS

I love the idea of rolling up thinly cut veggies and stuffing them in place of pasta. Everywhere I go these days I hear "gluten-free this" and "gluten-free that." This is a great option. It's also just a really nice dish. Zucchini are nice and small and two or three rolls make a perfect appetizer, but if you wanted to do this as an entrée, you could use eggplant for a larger portion. Any way you slice it, these look cute and elegant—and most important, they're delicious.

MISE EN PLACE

FOR THE CANNELLONI

3 medium zucchini

Kosher salt

Extra virgin olive oil

2 cloves garlic, smashed

Pinch of crushed red pepper

1 cup Homemade Ricotta (page 163) or store-bought

1 cup grated Parmigiano, plus more for garnish

1 bunch of fresh basil, leaves cut into a chiffonade

FOR THE SAUCE

Extra virgin olive oil

½ onion, cut into ¼-inch dice

Kosher salt

Pinch of crushed red pepper

2 cloves garlic, finely chopped

3 large beefsteak tomatoes, cored, seeded, and cut into ¼-inch dice

1 cup baby arugula

ANNE-NOTATION A mandoline is essential for success in this recipe. Also, you can make your own Homemade Ricotta, but store-bought is just fine.

FOR THE CANNELLONI

1 Remove one-third off one long side of each squash, to expose a long, wide, flat area. Using a mandoline, cut the zucchini lengthwise into wide, flat ⅛-inch-thick slices. The goal is to get 12 of the widest slices possible, so be choosy and use the middle of the zucchini for this—a couple extra slices for safety never hurts.

2 Cut the remaining rounded edge pieces of zucchini into ¼-inch dice.

3 Bring a medium saucepan of well-salted water to a boil.

4 Coat a large sauté pan with olive oil and toss in the 2 garlic cloves and crushed red pepper. Bring the pan to medium-high heat. When the garlic is golden and very aromatic, 1 to

(recipe continues)

★ ★
★

2 minutes, remove it and ditch it—it has fulfilled its garlic destiny. Add the diced zucchini, season with salt, and cook for 3 to 4 minutes, or until the zucchini begins to soften. Transfer the zucchini to a medium mixing bowl and let cool.

5   Working in batches, cook the zucchini slices in the salted boiling water for 1 minute or until they begin to soften. Use a slotted spoon to remove the slices from the water and lay them out on a baking sheet to cool.

6   When the diced zucchini is cool, stir in the ricotta, Parm, and half the basil. Taste and season with salt if needed . . . it probably will be.

7   Pat the zucchini slices dry with paper towels and lay them on a work surface. Spoon 1 tablespoon of the ricotta mixture on the end of each slice, carefully roll up the slices, return them to the baking sheet, and reserve.

FOR THE SAUCE

1   Coat a large sauté pan with olive oil and toss in the onion. Season with salt and crushed red pepper and bring the pan to medium heat. Cook until the onion is soft and aromatic, 6 to 8 minutes. Toss in the garlic and cook for 1 to 2 more minutes.

2   Stir in the tomatoes and season with salt. Continue to cook for another

8 to 10 minutes. Taste and adjust the seasoning if needed. Toss in the remaining basil and reserve.

TO ASSEMBLE

1   Preheat the oven to 350°F.

2   Put the zucchini "roll-ups" in the oven for 10 minutes or until just warmed through.

3   Place the tomato sauce over medium heat to warm.

4   In a small bowl, toss the arugula with a little olive oil and salt. Arrange the arugula in the center of 4 serving plates. Lay 3 zucchini rolls in a line on top of each arugula pile and spoon the sauce over the zucchini. Top with Parmigiano and serve.

un cannily good cannelloni!!

ricotta flan

with bacon, corn, cherry tomatoes, and arugula pesto

SERVES 6 TIME **ABOUT 1 HOUR**

Ricotta cheese is usually a supporting character. But this lovely little flan says, "Hi, ricotta, you shy girl, come out and be the superstar! Today's your day to shine." Honestly, I never thought that much about ricotta until I was traveling in Italy and ate "just made" ricotta—it was totally transporting. The pure, sweet milk flavor brought the joys of ricotta home to me! I suggest you try my Homemade Ricotta, or if you ever come across sheep's-milk ricotta, use that—it's very special and delightfully tangy. The delicate creamy flavor of the cheese is beautiful with summer's best sweet corn, juicy tomatoes, and peppery arugula. But the flan itself is so subtle you can think of it as a blank canvas—use whatever veggies float your boat.

MISE EN PLACE

FOR THE FLAN

Extra virgin olive oil

1/2 cup heavy cream

2 large eggs, beaten

2 cups Homemade Ricotta (page 163) or store-bought

1 teaspoon fresh lemon juice

Pinch of nutmeg

FOR THE SALAD

2 ears of corn, shucked

Extra virgin olive oil

4 slices bacon, cut into lardons

1/2 pint cherry tomatoes, halved

Kosher salt

Pinch of crushed red pepper

2 to 3 tablespoons red wine vinegar

1 cup baby arugula

FOR THE PESTO

1 1/2 cups baby arugula

2 tablespoons pine nuts

2 tablespoons grated Parmigiano

Big fat finishing oil

ANNE-NOTATION I find the easiest and least messy way to remove corn kernels from the cob is to chop one end off the cob to create a flat surface, put the cob in a large bowl with the flat bit sitting on the bottom of the bowl, and then shave the kernels off the cob—they fall right into the bowl. Pretty quick and easy (Q&E)!

FOR THE FLAN

1   Preheat the oven to 325°F. Generously brush 6 ramekins with olive oil and set aside.

(recipe continues)

2   Put the cream in a small saucepan over medium-high heat. Heat the cream until very hot but not boiling. Turn off the heat and whisk in the eggs. Add the ricotta, lemon juice, and nutmeg and stir to combine well.

3   Divide the flan mixture among the prepared ramekins. Place the ramekins in a baking dish and fill the dish with HOT tap water until it comes halfway up the sides of the ramekins. Cover the entire baking dish with foil and bake for 40 minutes, or until the flans are just set. Remove from the oven, discard the foil, and transfer to a rack to cool.

FOR THE SALAD

1   Preheat a grill or grill pan. Brush the corn with olive oil and cook until charred on all sides, about 10 minutes. Remove the corn from the grill, let cool, and cut the kernels off the cobs. Ditch the cobs and reserve the kernels.

2   Toss the bacon into a large sauté pan along with a few drops of olive oil. Bring the pan to medium heat and cook the bacon until it's brown and crispy, 7 to 8 minutes. Add the corn and tomatoes, and season with salt

and crushed red pepper. Cook for 3 to 4 minutes, or until the tomatoes just start to soften.

3   Stir in the red wine vinegar. Taste and reseason if needed.

FOR THE PESTO

In a blender, combine the arugula, pine nuts, and Parmigiano. Turn on the machine and drizzle in about $1/3$ cup of big fat finishing oil, enough to create a mixture that can be easily poured. Taste and season with salt if needed.

TO ASSEMBLE

1   Warm the flans in a 200°F. oven for 8 to 10 minutes.

2   Gently schmear serving plates with the arugula pesto. Unmold the flans on top of the pesto. (You might need to run a knife around the edges of the flans to release them.) Spoon some of the corn mixture over each flan, add a few leaves of arugula, and drizzle with any leftover pesto.

now that's fLAN-tastic!!!

pork and potato empanadas
with charred tomatillo sauce

SERVES **4 TO 8**   TIME **ABOUT 3 HOURS**

Almost every cuisine has its version of stuffed dough: there are empanadas, ravioli, pierogi, wontons, and more. I've had many versions; I think this one is a sort of cultural collaboration. It has a bit of Puerto Rico in it, some Mexican flavors, and definitely some Spanish influence—especially when it comes to the dipping sauce. For me, you can put anything in dough and fry, bake, or boil it and it's game on. Making and cooking dough takes some practice and patience, however, once you get the hang of it, I think you'll find the process fun and satisfying. Guess what else? The sauce is also SUPER yummy on tacos or as a dip for tortilla chips!

MISE EN PLACE

FOR THE DOUGH

1$1/4$ cups all-purpose flour, plus more as needed

1 teaspoon kosher salt

$1/4$ pound cold lard, cut into pea-size pieces

1 large egg yolk

1 tablespoon white vinegar

2 to 3 tablespoons ice water

2 large eggs beaten together with 2 tablespoons water

FOR THE FILLING

Extra virgin olive oil

2 pounds pork shoulder, cut into $1/2$-inch dice

2 teaspoons cumin seed, toasted and finely ground

$1/4$ cup all-purpose flour

Kosher salt

1 onion, cut into $1/4$-inch dice

1 poblano pepper, stemmed, seeded, and cut into $1/4$-inch dice

2 cloves garlic, smashed and finely chopped

3 large Yukon gold potatoes, cut into $1/4$-inch dice

$1/2$ bunch of fresh cilantro, leaves and stems finely chopped

2 bay leaves

$1/2$ cup dry white wine

2 cups chicken stock

FOR THE TOMATILLO SAUCE

6 tomatillos, husks removed

Extra virgin olive oil

2 cloves garlic, smashed and finely chopped

1 jalapeño, stemmed, seeded, and cut into $1/4$-inch dice

$1/2$ bunch of fresh cilantro, leaves and stems finely chopped

Kosher salt

Zest and juice of 1 large lime

(recipe continues) ★★★

TO MAKE THE DOUGH

1   In the bowl of a food processor, combine the flour, salt, and lard. Pulse, pulse, pulse until the mixture resembles grated Parmigiano.

2   Add the egg yolk, vinegar, and 1 tablespoon of the ice water. Pulse, pulse, pulse a few more times until the dough starts to come together. If the mix seems dry, add another 1 or 2 tablespoons ice water and pulse a couple more times—OR, if the mixture seems wet, add a little more flour. Flour is temperamental—some days you might need to add water, some days you might need to add flour. Accept it and move on.

3   Turn the dough out on a lightly floured work surface and squish it to bring it together into a ball. Knead the dough 2 or 3 times or until smooth. Form the dough into a flat disk, wrap it in plastic, put it in the fridge, and let it hang out for at least 1 hour. **HINT, HINT:** This totally can be a do-ahead; just let the dough come to room temp for 15 minutes before using.

TO MAKE THE FILLING

1   Coat a large wide pot with olive oil and bring to medium-high heat.

2   In a large bowl, toss the pork with the cumin, flour, and some salt.

3   Working in batches, brown the pork really well on all sides. Don't rush this step, it may take 6 to 7 minutes per batch. It's SUPER important NOT to crowd the pan—make sure the pan is hot and put only a single layer of pork in the pan at a time. If the pan is crowded, the pork will just steam and the flour will get mealy rather than brown and crispy. The browning is essential to building a deep, rich flavor. Brown food tastes good!!! Repeat the process until all the meat is browned, adding more oil as needed. If the bottom of the pan starts to burn, reduce the heat. If the pan does burn, stop, ditch the fat, wash the pan, and start over.

4   When the meat is well browned, ditch the oil in the pan and start with fresh oil. Bring the pan to medium heat, add the onion, and season with salt. Cook the onion for 4 to 5 minutes. Toss in the poblano and cook for another 3 to 4 minutes. Add the garlic and cook for another minute.

5   Return the pork to the pan with the veggies, toss in the potatoes, season with salt, and stir to combine. Add the cilantro and bay leaves. Add the wine and scrape the crud off the bottom of the pan. Add the chicken stock. Taste and season if needed. Bring the mixture to a boil and reduce to a simmer (BTB, RTS). Partially cover and simmer until the pork is tender, 35 to 40 minutes, adding a little more stock or water if the liquid cooks away and the mixture seems dry.

6 Remove the lid and cook, stirring frequently, until most of the liquid has reduced, 5 to 7 minutes. The mixture should be saucy, but not soupy. Taste and reseason if needed. Let the mixture cool completely. Remove and discard the bay leaves. **HINT, HINT:** Hello!!! This can also be a do-ahead!

TO MAKE THE TOMATILLO SAUCE

1 Preheat the grill or a grill pan to high heat. Place the tomatillos directly on the grill and cook on all sides until charred, 6 to 7 minutes. Remove and let cool. When the tomatillos are cool enough to handle, coarsely chop them.

2 Coat a large sauté pan with olive oil and bring to medium heat. Add the garlic, jalapeño, and half the cilantro and cook for 2 minutes.

3 Add the tomatillos to the pan, season with salt, and stir to combine. Taste and reseason if needed. Cook the tomatillos, stirring occasionally, for 7 to 8 minutes. Turn off the heat and add the lime zest and juice and the remaining cilantro.

4 Transfer the mix to a food processor and purée until smooth. Taste to make sure it is delicious. Reserve. **HINT, HINT:** Guess what? This can be a total do-ahead too!

TO ASSEMBLE THE EMPANADAS

1 Remove the dough from the fridge and let warm up for about 10 minutes. Preheat the oven to 400°F.

2 Dust a work surface lightly with flour and divide the dough into 8 equal parts. Roll each piece of dough into a ball. Using the palm of your hand, squash each dough ball to flatten it. With a rolling pin, roll each piece into a 6-inch circle.

3 Lay all of the circles out on the work surface. Spoon a generous mound of filling onto the bottom half of each dough circle, leaving a 1-inch rim along the bottom edge. Brush the bottom edge of each circle with the egg wash and fold the top half of the dough over the filling so it reaches about $1/2$ inch from the edge—you don't want the edges to match up exactly. Fold the bottom rim up over the top edge and crimp in a pretty way to seal the deal. Use a spatula to transfer the empanadas to a baking sheet. Brush the tops with the remaining egg wash.

4 Transfer the baking sheet to the oven and bake the empanadas for 25 to 30 minutes or until golden brown and shiny, rotating the tray halfway through the cooking time. Check the bottoms to make sure they are cooked through. Serve immediately with the tomatillo sauce.

Cute little empanadas!

bacalao fritters
with piquillo pepper
and marcona almond sauce

MAKES **ABOUT 36 FRITTERS**
TIME **ABOUT 1½ HOURS PLUS OVERNIGHT SOAKING OF THE COD**

Salted cod or bacalao, in Spanish, was historically prepared to preserve the fish before there was refrigeration. Now we just use it because we like it. It's very common in the Mediterranean, and working in Italian kitchens I've spent a lot of time making bacalao. Then when I was in Spain with my mom and sister, we had bacalao fritters. I remember sitting with them looking over the ocean, sipping chilly white wine, and happily popping these fritters in my mouth. And now you can, too!

MISE EN PLACE

FOR THE FRITTERS

1 pound salted dried cod, soaked 24 hours in water (change the water 3 times)

7 cloves garlic, smashed

2 cups whole milk

2 bay leaves

1 thyme bundle

3 large Yukon gold potatoes, cut into 12 even pieces

Kosher salt

2 cups all-purpose flour

2 eggs, beaten with 2 tablespoons water

2 cups panko bread crumbs

Peanut or other neutral-flavored oil for frying

FOR THE SAUCE

Extra virgin olive oil

3 cloves garlic, smashed

¾ cup Marcona almonds, coarsely chopped

2 pinches of crushed red pepper

1 12-ounce jar piquillo peppers, coarsely chopped

Kosher salt

¼ cup sherry vinegar

1 bunch of fresh chives, finely chopped

ANNE ALERT You need to soak the salted cod for 24 hours, so plan ahead!

FOR THE FRITTERS

1   In a medium saucepan, combine the soaked cod, 5 of the garlic cloves, the milk, bay leaves, thyme bundle, and

2 cups water. Bring the liquid to a boil and reduce to a simmer (BTB, RTS). Cook for 45 minutes to 1 hour, or until the cod flakes apart.

2   Put the potatoes in a medium saucepan and cover with water by

(recipe continues)

at least an inch. Toss in the remaining garlic, season the water with salt, and bring to a boil. Cook the potatoes until they are fork-tender, 20 to 25 minutes. Let cool and reserve.

3   Strain the cod through a mesh strainer. Discard the bay leaves and thyme bundle. Transfer the cod, garlic, and any milk curds to the bowl of a mixer outfitted with a paddle attachment. Beat the cod on low until broken up into small pieces and reserve.

4   Pass the cooked potatoes through a food mill and add them to the bowl with the cod. Beat slowly until combined. Taste and season with salt if needed.

5   Roll the mixture into 1-inch balls and reserve on a baking sheet.

6   Set up your standard breading procedure: 1 bowl of flour, 1 bowl with the egg-water mixture, and 1 bowl of bread crumbs. Using one hand for dry things and one hand for wet things, run each cod ball through the flour, shaking off any excess, then coat the balls in the egg mixture, then the panko. Reserve the breaded "fritters" on a baking sheet in the fridge until ready to fry.

7   Fill a wide, deep pan with about 2 inches of oil. Heat the oil to 350°F.

or until it sizzles when you flick a bit of flour or bread crumbs into it.

8   Set up a drying situation next to the stove by lining a baking sheet with paper towels. Working in batches, add the fritters to the hot oil and fry until brown and crispy on all sides. Be sure not to crowd the pan, and reduce the heat if the oil starts to smoke. When the fritters are done, transfer them to the paper towels and immediately sprinkle with salt.

FOR THE SAUCE

1   Coat a large sauté pan with olive oil. Add the garlic, almonds, and crushed red pepper and bring the pan to medium heat. Cook the garlic and almonds for 3 to 4 minutes, or until aromatic and golden. Toss in the piquillo peppers and season with salt. Add the sherry vinegar and cook until it has reduced by half, about 2 minutes.

2   Transfer the mixture to a food processor and purée until it's smoothish—it should still have some texture. Taste, season with salt if needed, transfer to a serving bowl, and sprinkle with chives. Serve with the warm fritters.

baca- loooove!!!

homemade pita bread

with pickled feta spread

SERVES 4 TO 6 TIME ABOUT 3 HOURS, UNATTENDED

I eat at a lot of places where my friends are chefs, so I eat tons of really delicious and inspired food. Every now and then I taste something and I want to steal the idea. This recipe is a riff on a dish created by my friend Koren Grieveson when she was the chef at Avec restaurant in Chicago. It takes two of my favorite flavor oppositions—salt and vinegar—and marries them in a delicious creamy spread. It's amazing. First you taste it and say, "Yum!" and then you say, "Who knew you could pickle cheese???"

MISE EN PLACE

FOR THE PITA

1 ¼-ounce package active dry yeast

1 teaspoon sugar

1¼ cups warm water

1½ cups bread flour, plus more as needed

1½ cups whole wheat flour

1 teaspoon kosher salt

1 teaspoon cumin seed, toasted and ground

Pinch of cayenne pepper

¼ cup extra virgin olive oil, plus more for the bowl

FOR THE FETA

1 cup champagne vinegar

1 bunch of fresh mint

1 bay leaf

2 tablespoons sugar

2 teaspoons kosher salt

4 sprigs of fresh dill, leaves finely chopped and stems reserved

½ pound feta cheese, coarsely crumbled

½ cup Greek yogurt

FOR THE PITA

1   In a small bowl, combine the yeast, sugar, and warm water. Let sit for 15 minutes.

2   In a large bowl, combine the bread flour, whole wheat flour, salt, cumin, and cayenne. Make a well in the center of the dry ingredients and add the liquid mixture and the olive oil. Stir until the dough comes together.

3   Dust a work surface lightly with flour and knead the dough for 10 to 12 minutes or until it is firm and not at all sticky or tacky.

4   Oil a large bowl, add the dough, cover with plastic wrap, and put in a warm place for about 1½ hours, until the dough doubles in size.

FOR THE FETA

1   Combine the vinegar, mint, bay leaf, sugar, salt, and dill stems in a small saucepan with 1 cup water. Turn the heat to medium and simmer until the sugar and salt dissolve, 1 to 2 minutes. Remove from the heat and let cool.

(recipe continues)

2   Combine the feta cheese and the pickling liquid in a container, making sure the feta is fully submerged in the liquid.

3   Let the feta sit in the pickling liquid for at least 2 hours in the fridge but preferably overnight.

4   Strain the feta from the pickling liquid. Transfer the cheese to a food processor, and purée with the yogurt until smooth. Transfer the mixture to a serving container and sprinkle with the chopped dill.

TO BAKE THE PITA

1   Arrange an oven rack in the lowest possible position. Preheat the oven to 500°F.

2   Transfer the dough to a lightly floured surface, divide it into 8 equal pieces, then roll each piece into a 7-inch disk about ¼ inch thick.

3   Transfer the disks to baking sheets, cover them loosely with tea towels so they don't dry out, and let them hang out for 20 minutes at room temperature.

4   Place one baking sheet on the lowest rack and bake the pitas for 3 to 4 minutes. Flip the pitas and bake for another 2 minutes, or until puffed and lightly browned. Repeat with the remaining baking sheets.

5   Let cool and cut into triangles. Serve with the pickled feta.

ANNE-NOTATION The feta is best when pickled overnight, so plan ahead. If you're in a pinch, you can let it sit for just a couple of hours, but the tangy, zesty flavor is more vibrant the longer it sits.

pita picked a pickled feta ...

Rack of Lamb with Harissa

seconds

garlic chicken
with israeli couscous   67

pollo a mattone   69

braised chicken
with pomegranate molasses   73

west indian chicken
roti   75

seared duck breasts
with grape sauce   79

cornish game hens
with pancetta rosemary crust   80

big brined herby
turkey   83

balsamic-braised
beef brisket
with bacon and mushrooms   86

grilled hanger steak
with bagna cauda sauce   89

shepherd's pie   92

hawaiian pork roast   95

mustard-braised pork
shoulder   98

rack of lamb
with harissa   100

pork porterhouse
with apple, prune, and saba sauce   102

braised pork belly
with cumin and ginger   105

girl chef's grilled
lobster   108

crispy skate
in "crazy water"   111

fish and chips   114

seared wild striped bass
with fennel, pink grapefruit, and
dandelion   117

whole roasted fish
in salt crust   120

olive oil–poached salmon
with kumquat compote   122

squid fideua
with aïoli   123

I find that most chefs consider the entrée

to be the main attraction. I'm not really one of those chefs. I like main courses, but my issue with mains is that traditionally they revolve around a big hunk of protein and some veg and some starch . . . blah blah blah. Don't get me wrong, I'm a huge fan of BIG MEAT, but sometimes it's a little more challenging to get creative when it comes to second courses. How many different ways can you cook a pork chop, right?

However, once I started broadening my horizons and exploring and experimenting with different flavor profiles—using ingredients outside my rustic Italian repertoire—I began to think about the main course in a whole new way. Suddenly there were tons of ways to flavor a pork chop, to marinate a steak, or to season a chicken that I'd never thought of. I definitely still have one foot planted firmly in my rustic Italian kitchen, but there are lots of other ingredients that I had tasted along the way, but hadn't integrated into my own cooking. Expanding beyond my roots was a big step in terms of rediscovering my love of mains! Of course, the cooking techniques are the ones I've always relied on—brining, marinating, dry-rubbing, grilling, roasting, braising, searing, frying. All those skills are the same, but the dishes themselves take on totally different personalities now that I've branched out of my comfort zone and play with different ingredients and flavor combos.

So try it! Take a different direction tonight when you're shopping for dinner. All the basic cooking techniques are right here in this book, and once you know them, I bet you'll feel totally empowered using them to explore different flavors and types of food. Jump out there and be more adventurous with herbs, spices, and flavor combos. The confidence starts with understanding how to cook, and the fun continues when you begin to dive into new tastes and combinations. As the chef of your own kitchen, you can do exactly what I do—get inspired by the food you taste when you eat out, when you travel, or when you read a cookbook. Then go for it! Start with these recipes that have totally turned me on and get ready to love seconds as much as I do. YEAH!

garlic chicken
with israeli couscous

SERVES 4   TIME **ABOUT 4 HOURS**

Growing up in upstate New York there were always casseroles being trucked around—for every occasion someone would show up with a casserole and then there was the inevitable, "I have to return the casserole dish." Maybe that's where I got the inspiration for this dish . . . my "upscale casserole." Give a chicken a little roasted garlic rubdown and toss it in a pot—what's not to love?

MISE EN PLACE

FOR THE CHICKEN

2 whole garlic bulbs

Grated zest and juice of
   1 lemon

1 tablespoon cumin seed,
   toasted and ground

Pinch of crushed
   red pepper

Kosher salt

Extra virgin olive oil

1 4-pound chicken, cut into
   8 to 10 pieces

FOR THE ISRAELI COUSCOUS

Kosher salt

2 cups Israeli couscous

Extra virgin olive oil

1 onion, sliced

4 celery ribs, sliced thinly
   on a severe bias

Pinch of crushed
   red pepper

1/2 cup tomato paste

1 cup dry white wine

1 large pinch of saffron

2 medium zucchini, green
   part only (discard the
   starchy, seedy center),
   cut into 1/2-inch dice

1/2 cup pine nuts, toasted

1 thyme bundle

1 bay leaf

1 1/2 to 2 cups chicken stock

4 scallions, white and green
   parts, sliced very thinly
   on the bias

1 bunch of fresh cilantro,
   leaves and stems finely
   chopped, plus a few
   whole leaves for garnish

FOR THE CHICKEN

1   Preheat the oven to 375°F.

2   Place the garlic bulbs in the oven and roast until soft, about 30 minutes. Remove and let cool. When the bulbs are cool enough to handle, slice off the tops and squeeze the cloves into the bowl of a food processor.

3   Add the lemon zest and juice, cumin, and crushed red pepper to the garlic. Season the mixture with salt

and purée until smooth. While the machine is running, drizzle in 1/4 cup olive oil. Taste and reseason if needed.

4   Place the chicken in a large dish or on a baking sheet and massage the garlic mixture onto the skin of each piece—really lube it up! Let the chicken sit at room temp for up to 2 hours or, if longer than 2 hours, in the fridge. **HINT, HINT:** This can be done WAY ahead of time!

(recipe continues)

FOR THE COUSCOUS

1   Bring a medium pot of salted water to a boil—taste the water to make sure it is salty like the ocean! Add the couscous and cook until it's two-thirds of the way done, 5 to 6 minutes. Strain and reserve.

2   Coat a large sauté pan with olive oil, toss in the onion and celery, and bring to medium-high heat. Season with salt and crushed red pepper and cook until soft, 7 to 8 minutes.

3   Stir in the tomato paste, white wine, and saffron and cook for 3 to 4 more minutes.

4   Toss in the zucchini, reserved couscous, pine nuts, thyme bundle, and bay leaf and stir to combine. Add $1^1/_2$ cups chicken stock and stir. The couscous should be a little soupy. If it isn't, add the remaining $^1/_2$ cup chicken stock. Taste and reseason if needed. Remove and discard the bay leaf and the thyme bundle. Transfer the mixture to a large baking dish— one big enough to hold the chicken as well—and reserve.

TO ASSEMBLE

1   Preheat the oven to 375°F.

2   Coat a large sauté pan with olive oil and bring it to medium-high heat. Working in batches, brown the chicken on all sides. Be patient, this may take up to 6 to 8 minutes. BE SURE not to crowd the pan. If you do, the chicken will steam and get soggy rather than brown and crispy . . . not yummy.

3   Nestle the browned chicken skin side up in the prepared couscous. Cover with foil and place in the oven. Roast the chicken for 20 minutes, remove the foil, and roast for another 15 minutes.

4   When the chicken is cooked through, remove from the oven and top with the chopped scallions and cilantro to serve.

tastes like GARLIC chicken!

pollo a mattone

SERVES 4   TIME **ABOUT 3 HOURS**

Leave it to Italians to come up with the idea of cooking a chicken under a brick—it's like chicken roadkill! First, you take out the backbone and the rib cage. I like to tie the legs together to make it look a bit more presentable. You can do this with either a regular chicken or a cute little Cornish hen. Once you take out the spine and weigh it down with a brick, it gets really flat so the skin gets super crispy, and it cooks very evenly. If you like crispy chicken skin, this is the recipe for you! These days you can buy a special terra-cotta chicken squasher, but I just wrap a brick in aluminum foil and toss it on top of the bird. I wonder if it was an accident the first time they made this dish. Did something heavy fall on the chicken and someone said, "Hey, crispy flat chicken—now that's a great idea!"

MISE EN PLACE

4 cloves garlic, smashed and finely chopped

Grated zest and juice of 1 lemon

½ teaspoon crushed red pepper

2 sprigs of fresh rosemary, leaves finely chopped

1 teaspoon pimenton (smoked paprika)

1 teaspoon cumin seed, toasted and finely ground

Kosher salt

Extra virgin olive oil

2 3-pound chickens, backbone and rib cage removed

½ cup dry white wine

1 cup chicken stock

ANNE-NOTATION For this recipe you'll need a brick covered in aluminum foil.

1   In a small bowl, combine the garlic, lemon zest and juice, crushed red pepper, rosemary, pimenton, cumin, and salt. Add just enough olive oil to create a loose paste.

2   Tie the chickens' legs together with butcher's twine—this makes for a nicer presentation. Massage the paste of garlic deliciousness all over the chickens, cover, and let sit for up to 2 hours at room temp (if marinating longer than 2 hours, put them in the fridge, but be sure to bring them back to room temp before cooking).

3   Preheat the oven to 375°F. and wrap a brick in aluminum foil.

4   Coat the bottom of a large sauté pan with olive oil and bring to high heat. Working one chicken at a time, lay the marinated chicken skin side down in the preheated pan—be sure to put the skin side down first to create a REALLY lovely, crispy, flavorful chicken skin.

5   Lay the wrapped brick directly on top of the chicken to really squash it down and flatten it—this helps the chicken cook evenly and creates

(recipe continues)

a crispy skin—and cook for 5 to 6 minutes. Remove the brick, turn over the chicken, and cook for another 3 to 4 minutes. Transfer the chicken to a rimmed baking sheet and reserve. Ditch the oil in the pan, wipe out the pan, add fresh oil, and repeat this process with the other chicken. Reserve the pan that the chickens have been browned in and SAVE THE CRUD (the brown stuff on the bottom of the pan). It tastes good!

6   Transfer the chickens to the oven and roast for 18 to 20 minutes or until cooked through. Remove and let rest for 8 to 10 minutes.

7   While the chickens roast, ditch the oil from the sauté pan and add the wine. Bring the pan to medium heat and use a wooden spoon to scrape the beautiful brown crud off the bottom of the pan. Continue cooking until the wine has reduced by about three-quarters. Add the chicken stock, season with salt, and cook until evaporated by half. Taste to make sure the sauce is delicious and reseason if needed. This sauce will not be thick like gravy, so don't sweat it.

8   Remove the twine from the chicken legs and discard—no need to floss and eat at the same time! Split the chickens in half lengthwise, transfer each half to a plate, and drizzle with the sauce to serve.

she's a brick house . . .

own your chicken

Another name for butterflying a bird is spatchcocking. That makes me giggle every time I say it, but quite honestly, it's one of my favorite ways to prepare a chicken.

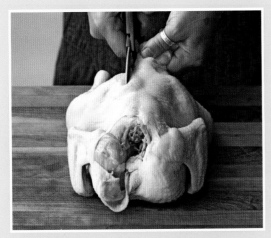

Using poultry shears, find the backbone of the chicken. If you're not sure which is the back, poke it—the breasts are soft. If you poke this side, turn it over, the other side will feel bony. That's the back.

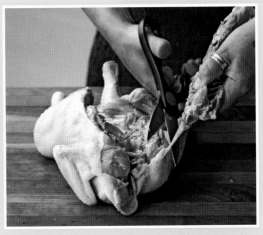

Take the shears and cut right up one side of the spine and down the other—this is totally empowering!

Open up the chicken like a book. Using a sharp boning knife, keep the blade on the bone and run it right underneath the bone in long, smooth strokes to carefully free it from the meat. Try not to dig into the meat, that's the big-money item.

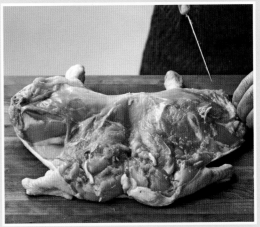

Do this with both sides of the rib cage and then just pull out the breastbone—the cartilage right in the center.

Guess what? You've just spatchcocked your bird!

braised chicken
with pomegranate molasses

SERVES 4 TIME **ABOUT 45 MINUTES**

I'm crazy for pomegranate molasses. I first discovered it when I was working at a restaurant in SoHo, and one of my tasks was to make the spice run (that was just because I lived near the store). It was such a treat—I'd get sent up to Kalustyan's, an incredible Indian spice market, to shop for ingredients for the restaurant. I'd go upstairs to where they serve food and get a falafel and hummus sandwich and then wander through the aisles of spices, rice, sweets, and grains, just taking it all in, amazed by the array of flavors the world has to offer. One of these was pomegranate molasses. Pomegranate is actually used a lot in Italian cooking, so I felt comfy using this delicious delicacy! It's a brilliant red color, has a lovely jammy consistency, and it's super sour, so it gives dishes a real flavor bump. I love shellacking it on the outside of a chicken for a tangy, tart, sticky glaze.

MISE EN PLACE

Extra virgin olive oil

4 cloves garlic, smashed

Crushed red pepper

8 chicken thighs, trimmed of excess skin

Kosher salt

1 cup pomegranate molasses

1 cup chicken stock

1 thyme bundle

1 cup pomegranate seeds

1 bunch of fresh chives, finely chopped

1 Preheat the oven to 350°F.

2 Coat a large sauté pan with olive oil. Toss in 2 of the garlic cloves and a pinch of crushed red pepper. Bring the pan to medium-high heat. When the garlic is golden and very aromatic, remove it and discard—it has fulfilled its garlic destiny.

3 Season the chicken thighs with salt and place them skin side down in the pan. Don't crowd the pan or the thighs will steam instead of brown—you may have to work in batches here, NO WORRIES. Brown the chicken thighs really well on both sides, 10 to 12 minutes total. Transfer the thighs to a rimmed baking sheet and reserve.

4 Ditch the oil from the pan and add $\frac{1}{2}$ cup of the pomegranate molasses along with $\frac{1}{4}$ cup of the chicken stock. Bring the mixture to a boil and let it evaporate by half—it should be slightly thick and syrupy.

(recipe continues)

5   Return the chicken to the pan, reduce the heat to medium, and cook in the sauce for 1 to 2 minutes on each side, or until it clings to the chicken in a yummy embrace.

6   Transfer the chicken to the baking sheet and roast for 10 to 12 minutes or until cooked through.

7   While the chicken roasts, add the remaining molasses, stock, and garlic to the pan along with the thyme bundle and a pinch of crushed red pepper. Taste and season with salt if needed. Bring to a boil and reduce to a simmer (BTB, RTS). Cook until the liquid is thick and syrupy. Discard the garlic cloves and thyme bundle.

8   Remove the chicken from the oven, transfer to a serving dish, drizzle with the sauce, and sprinkle with the pomegranate seeds and chives before serving.

now that's a chick i'll stick with!

west indian chicken roti

SERVES 6 TIME **ABOUT 3 HOURS**

I've been to the British Virgin Islands on a couple of occasions for food and wine festivals, and it's always been incredible. Of course we chefs worked hard, but whenever we'd get a break, some of us would take off for lunch and go to road-house shacks to try the local fare. We'd grab a big rum drink and then hoover these unbelievable chicken roti—another version of yummy stuff in dough. Then, when we had the occasional night off, we'd go out looking for food as interesting and delicious as those roti, but there didn't seem to be anything available except touristy food. I finally learned that the roti are made for the local workers to eat at lunch. At night the locals are all home eating dinner with their families. Only tourists in the know get to experience these yummy chicken roti instead of eating a burger or chicken salad!

MISE EN PLACE

FOR THE CHICKEN STEW

Vegetable oil

6 skinless, boneless chicken thighs, cut into 1/2-inch dice

Kosher salt

2 teaspoons all-purpose flour

1 onion, cut into 1/4-inch dice

2 celery ribs, cut into 1/4-inch dice

2 carrots, cut into 1/4-inch dice

2 cloves garlic, smashed and finely chopped

2 red jalapeño peppers, stem, seeds, and ribs removed, cut into 1/4-inch dice

3 Yukon gold potatoes, cut into 1/2-inch dice

1 13- to 15-ounce can unsweetened coconut milk

1 cup chicken stock

1 tablespoon curry powder

1 tablespoon turmeric

2 teaspoons cumin seed, toasted and finely ground

2 teaspoons coriander seed, toasted and finely ground

1/2 teaspoon cinnamon

1 teaspoon mustard seed

1/4 teaspoon cloves

1/4 teaspoon allspice

Grated zest and juice of 1 lime

1 tablespoon packed dark or light brown sugar

1 bay leaf

FOR THE ROTI

1 1/2 cups all-purpose flour, plus more as needed

1 cup whole wheat flour

1 teaspoon baking powder

Kosher salt

2 tablespoons vegetable oil, plus more for frying

1 large egg beaten with 1 tablespoon water

(recipe continues)

There are a lot of ingredients in this dish, but each one is important. They all come together to make a beautiful roti mosaic. It's totally worth the effort! Also, traditionally this dish is made with a habanero or Scotch bonnet pepper instead of a jalapeño, so if you want to go that way, knock yourself out—but proceed at your own risk.

FOR THE CHICKEN STEW

1 Coat a large, wide, straight-sided pan with vegetable oil and bring it to medium-high heat.

2 Season the chicken with salt and toss with the flour. Add half the chicken to the pan and brown it well on all sides, 4 to 5 minutes total. Remove the chicken from the pan and reserve. Ditch the oil from the pan, add fresh oil, and repeat the process with the remaining chicken. Ditch the oil again and add fresh oil.

3 Add the onion, celery, and carrots to the pan, season with salt, and cook until the veggies begin to soften, 5 to 6 minutes. Add the garlic and jalapeños and cook for 1 to 2 more minutes.

4 Return the chicken to the pan and add the potatoes, coconut milk, and half the chicken stock. Season with salt.

5 Add the curry powder, turmeric, cumin, coriander, cinnamon, mustard seed, cloves, allspice, lime zest and

juice, brown sugar, and bay leaf. Stir to combine and taste to make sure it's on the road to being delicious. Bring to a boil, reduce to a simmer (BTB, RTS), and cook the stew for 30 minutes, stirring occasionally. Taste and reseason if needed. Add the remaining chicken stock and simmer for another 15 minutes. Fish out the bay leaf and discard. The stew should be thick and really flavorful.

TO MAKE THE ROTI

1 Combine the all-purpose flour, whole wheat flour, baking powder, and a pinch of salt.

2 Make a hole in the center of the dry ingredients and add the 2 tablespoons oil and 1 cup water. Use a fork to combine. When the mixture comes together, turn the dough out onto a lightly floured work surface and knead 5 or 6 times, or until smooth. The dough should be fairly soft.

3 Return the dough to the bowl, cover with plastic wrap or a tea towel, and let it hang out for 15 to 20 minutes.

4 Divide the dough into 6 equal parts and roll into balls. On a lightly floured work surface, roll each ball out into an 8-inch circle $1/8$ to $1/4$ inch thick. Set the dough on a baking sheet with a layer of plastic wrap between each circle—don't forget this or the dough will stick together . . . that would suck!

gimme an umbrella drink!

TO ASSEMBLE

1   Preheat the oven to 200°F. Set up a baking sheet lined with paper towels next to the stove.

2   Lay each piece of dough on a clean work surface. Spoon the stew filling onto the bottom half of each circle, leaving a 1-inch rim along the bottom edge. Brush the bottom edge with the egg wash and fold the top half of the dough over the filling to meet the bottom. Crimp the edge with your fingers so it sticks together and looks pretty.

3   Add oil to a large sauté pan to a depth of $1/2$ inch and bring it to medium-high heat. Working in batches, use a large spatula to carefully place the roti in the oil and fry them on both sides until golden brown, 3 to 4 minutes per side. The dough will become delightfully bubbly and crispy. When they're done, carefully transfer the roti to the lined baking sheet and blot dry on both sides. Transfer to the oven to stay warm while you fry the remaining roti. Serve immediately and devour.

seared duck breasts
with grape sauce

SERVES 4 TIME ABOUT 1½ HOURS

When I'm wheeling through the greenmarket in the fall and I see all the grapes, it sends me back to Tuscany during the harvest season and wine-making time. So when sweater weather rolls around, I bundle up and buy a bounty of beautiful Concord or purple grapes—they're so small and plump and hugely flavorful—and combine them with wild game. It's the perfect gamey-grapey dinner!

MISE EN PLACE

4 duck breasts

Kosher salt

Extra virgin olive oil

2 cups seedless Concord or purple grapes

2 cups chicken stock

½ cup port

2 tablespoons red wine vinegar

½ bunch of fresh chives, finely chopped

1. Using a sharp paring knife, score the fat on the duck breasts to create a crosshatched pattern (be sure to cut all the way through the fat but not into the meat). Season with salt and let them hang out for about 15 minutes.

2. Preheat the oven to 350°F.

3. Add about 1 tablespoon olive oil to a large sauté pan. Place the duck skin side down and bring the pan to medium heat. Cook the duck low and slow to allow the fat to melt out. As the fat renders, spoon it from the pan and SAVE IT—it's perfect for frying potatoes! This process takes some patience, about 20 minutes, so don't rush it . . . you want nice, crispy duck skin.

4. When the skin is really crispy and brown, turn and cook for 2 to 3 minutes more to brown the other side.

5. Transfer the breasts to a rimmed baking sheet and roast for 5 to 6 minutes. Remove from the oven, cover loosely with foil, and let rest for 10 to 12 minutes—don't skip this step.

6. Add the grapes to the sauté pan along with ½ cup of the chicken stock and bring the pan to medium heat. Cook the grapes until they split and release their juices, about 10 minutes. Remove half the grapes from the pan and reserve.

7. Add the remaining chicken stock, port, and vinegar to the pan. Season with salt and cook until evaporated by half. Return the reserved grapes to the pan, taste, and reseason if needed.

8. Slice the duck breasts on the bias and garnish with the sauce and chives.

it's grraaaaape!

cornish game hens
with pancetta rosemary crust

SERVES 4 TIME ABOUT 1½ HOURS

I invented this recipe when I was working at a little Italian restaurant on the Upper East Side of Manhattan. It was a crappy little restaurant—my paycheck kept bouncing and I was totally frustrated and broke—so I left. But I took this recipe of mine with me! I turn pancetta—a delicious porky product—into a pâté of sorts and then use it as a crust for a lovely little Cornish game hen. It's like a pancetta cape for the chicken. It kind of turns a simple chicken into a super-chicken! Because the crust keeps all the moisture wrapped up inside the bird, you get a juicy and extremely flavorful result. Yum.

MISE EN PLACE

¾ pound pancetta, cut into ½-inch dice

4 Cornish game hens, backbone and rib cage removed

Extra virgin olive oil

Kosher salt

3 sprigs of fresh rosemary, leaves finely chopped

3 cloves garlic, smashed and finely chopped

½ teaspoon crushed red pepper

2 to 4 tablespoons ice water

½ cup dry white wine

1 cup chicken stock

2 tablespoons unsalted butter

1 Put the diced pancetta in the freezer for 30 minutes to partially freeze it. Preheat the oven to 375°F.

2 Tie the legs of each of the hens together with butcher's twine.

3 Coat a large sauté pan with olive oil and bring it to medium-high heat. Season both sides of the hens with salt and place them in the pan skin side down. Brown them really well on the first side, then flip them over and repeat with the second side—this will take 4 to 5 minutes per side. You will probably have to work in batches, one or two at a time. Do NOT crowd the pan—you want to get the hens really nice and brown. Brown food tastes good!!! Transfer the hens, skin side up, to a rimmed baking sheet and reserve. SAVE THE PAN but ditch the fat—in other words, don't wash the pan! It has lovely brown crud on the bottom that will be used to make a little pan sauce.

4 In a food processor combine the frozen pancetta, rosemary, garlic, and crushed red pepper. Purée the mixture until it starts to look like a paste, stopping periodically as needed to scrape the pancetta chunks from the sides with a rubber spatula.

★ ★
(recipe continues) ★

When the mixture starts to look smooth, keep the machine running and add a couple tablespoons of ice water to the mix. Continue to purée until the mixture looks *really* smooth. If needed, add a little more ice water, 3 to 4 tablespoons in total.

5   Schmear the pancetta mixture all over the skin side of the hens, and BE SURE to really stick it on in an even layer. Transfer the pancetta-crusted hens to the oven and roast for 25 minutes.

6   While the hens cook, return the sauté pan to a burner and pour in the white wine. Bring the pan to medium-high heat and scrape the brown bits off the bottom with a wooden spoon. Let the wine cook until only a couple tablespoons are left, then add the chicken stock and a little sprinkle of salt. Continue cooking until the liquid has evaporated by half. Add the butter in two pats, swirl it around, and turn off the heat. Taste to make sure it is delicious—it will be fairly acidic, and that's a GOOD THING!

7   Remove the hens from the oven, cut the butcher's twine off the legs, transfer to serving plates, and spoon the pan juices over the hens to serve.

now that's a SUPER chicken!

big brined herby turkey

SERVES 8 TO 10   TIME ABOUT 4 DAYS, MOSTLY UNATTENDED

I LOOOOOVE Thanksgiving dinner—so much so that I make the exact same dinner every year. I never, ever branch out and change it up. Why? Because if I'm going to cook it, I'm going to make what I like—my big brined turkey. At my Thanksgiving table the turkey is definitely the superstar—they don't call it Turkey Day for nothing! This is DEFINITELY a plan-ahead holiday dinner because I do the extend-o brine—I brine my bird for three days. I see these recipes that call for an overnight brining, or a few hours, and I say p-shaw! It takes three days to do the job right and that's how I do it. Gobble! Gobble!

MISE EN PLACE

FOR THE BRINE

3/4 cup kosher salt

1/3 cup sugar

2 onions, cut into 1/2-inch dice

2 carrots, cut into 1/2-inch dice

3 celery ribs, cut into 1/2-inch dice

1 whole garlic bulb, cut in half equatorially

1/2 bunch of fresh rosemary

1/2 bunch of fresh sage

2 tablespoons coriander seed

2 tablespoons fennel seed

6 bay leaves

1 teaspoon crushed red pepper

One 15-pound fresh turkey, neck and giblets reserved

FOR THE HERB BUTTER

1/2 pound (2 sticks) unsalted butter, at room temperature

1/2 bunch of fresh rosemary, leaves finely chopped

1/2 bunch of fresh sage, leaves finely chopped

Kosher salt

FOR THE GRAVY

2 onions, cut into 1/2-inch dice

2 carrots, cut into 1/2-inch dice

2 celery ribs, cut into 1/2-inch dice

4 cloves garlic, smashed

1 thyme bundle

3 bay leaves

Kosher salt

2 quarts chicken stock

3/4 cup all-purpose flour

2 cups dry white wine

ANNE ALERT With a three-day brine, this is DEFINITELY a think-ahead recipe. Which gives you plenty of time to make my favorite Sausage and Mushroom Stuffing (page 214 and my Cranberry-Clementine Chutney (page 225) to go with it!

TO BRINE THE TURKEY

In a container large enough to accommodate all the ingredients including the turkey, combine 2 gallons water with the salt, sugar, onions, carrots, celery, garlic,

(recipe continues)

rosemary, sage, coriander seed, fennel seed, bay leaves, and crushed red pepper. Stir to combine. Submerge the turkey in the brine. Cover and refrigerate for 3 days.

TO PREPARE THE TURKEY FOR ROASTING

1 The night before you are planning to roast the bird, remove it from the brine and pat it dry with paper towels.

2 In a small bowl, combine the butter, rosemary, sage, and some salt. Taste to make sure it is delicious.

3 Using your fingers, carefully work your way under the skin of the turkey to separate it from the breasts and legs. Massage the herb butter under the skin of the breast and legs, then all over the outside of the bird as well. This will act like suntan lotion to create a lovely crispy brown skin.

4 Tie the turkey's legs together with butcher's twine to create that perfect turkey shape. This will also keep the bird nice and compact for even cooking.

5 In the bottom of your roasting pan, for the gravy, combine the onions, carrots, celery, garlic, thyme bundle, and bay leaves. Season with salt.

6 Plunk the turkey on top of the veggies and put in the fridge overnight

uncovered. Yes, that's right . . . UNCOVERED. This allows the skin of the turkey to dry out and creates a gorgeous, brown, crispy skin. Now a bunch of your prep work is out of the way, so all you have to do tomorrow is toss the turkey in the oven!

TO ROAST THE TURKEY

1 Preheat the oven to 450°F.

2 Pour 2 cups of the chicken stock into the roasting pan and put the turkey in the screaming hot oven for 35 to 40 minutes, or until the turkey becomes beautifully browned.

3 Reduce the heat to 350°F. Baste the turkey with the pan juices and rotate the pan every 30 minutes for the remainder of the cooking time. Think 17 minutes per pound . . . you do the math. If the turkey starts to get too brown, tent it loosely with aluminum foil.

4 Remove the turkey from the oven when an instant-read thermometer registers 155°F. when inserted into the thickest part of the turkey (be sure the thermometer is not touching a bone or you'll get an inaccurate reading). Transfer your beautiful bird to a rimmed baking sheet, cover it loosely with aluminum foil, and let it rest for at least 30 minutes.

TO MAKE THE GRAVY

1   Using a mesh strainer, strain the veggies out of the cooking liquid over a large bowl and allow the fat to rise to the top of the cooking liquid. Discard the veggies. Save the roasting pan, but don't wash it—you still need it.

2   Skim the fat off the surface of the cooking liquid. Place the roasting pan directly on a burner, add the skimmed fat to the pan, and bring it to medium heat.

3   Whisk in the flour and cook the mixture until it has the consistency of wet sand. Whisk in the wine and cook for 4 to 5 minutes.

4   Add the reserved cooking juices and the remaining chicken stock to the flour mixture. Bring the liquid to a boil and reduce to a simmer (BTB, RTS). Cook until the mixture is the consistency of thick gravy, about 10 minutes. Taste and season with salt if needed.

5   Carve the turkey and serve with the gravy.

let's talk turkey...

balsamic-braised beef brisket
with bacon and mushrooms

SERVES **4 TO 6**   TIME **ABOUT 4 HOURS**

This is one of my favorites of all the recipes I've ever written. I first experienced braising with balsamic vinegar when I was in Italy. I think it was a veal shank—it was sweet, syrupy, sour, and oh-so-tender. I was amazed and I thought, "Wow, vinegar can taste like this?" So I applied the same technique to a brisket. With this combo you get BIG MEAT flavors plus the earthiness of mushrooms, all rounded out by the saltiness of some bacon. It's such a sexy dish. When I made it on *Secrets of a Restaurant Chef* I could barely wrap the show before the crew attacked me like a pack of wild dogs, because everyone wanted a bite of my brisket!

MISE EN PLACE

Extra virgin olive oil

1 5-pound beef brisket

Kosher salt

¼ pound slab bacon or 4 to 5 slices of bacon, cut into lardons

4 onions, thinly sliced

4 celery ribs, sliced thinly on the bias

4 cloves garlic, smashed and finely chopped

1½ pounds cremini mushrooms, stemmed and sliced

2 cups balsamic vinegar

3 cups chicken stock

1 thyme bundle

4 bay leaves

1 bunch fresh chives, finely chopped

ANNE ALERT This beautiful brisket needs time to braise, so plan ahead.

1   Preheat the oven to 375°F.

2   Coat a large, wide, shallow pan with olive oil and bring it to high heat.

3   Season the brisket generously with salt and add it to the pan. Brown the meat well on all sides, about 20 minutes total. Don't skimp on this step—BROWN FOOD tastes good.

Remove the brisket from the pan and reserve. Ditch the oil.

4   Add a few drops of fresh oil to the pan and toss in the bacon. Bring the pan to medium heat and cook until the bacon is brown and crispy, 6 to 7 minutes.

5   Toss in the onions, celery, and garlic and season with salt. Cook until the veggies are tender, 7 to 8 minutes.

(recipe continues)

6   Add the mushrooms and cook for 2 to 3 more minutes.

7   Add the balsamic vinegar and cook until evaporated by half, 5 to 6 minutes. Taste it—at this point it will be very vinegary—that's okay. Season with salt if needed. BTW: Salt offsets acid, so it will help take down the vinegar flavor a little bit.

8   Transfer the mixture to a roasting pan and lay the brisket on top. Add the chicken stock and jiggle the pan to nestle everyone together comfortably. Toss in the thyme bundle and bay leaves. Cover the pan with foil and place in the oven. Braise the brisket for 1 hour, then turn and braise for 1 more hour. Remove the foil and cook for 30 minutes more.

9   Remove the brisket from the oven, transfer to a cutting board, cover loosely with foil, and let rest for 20 minutes.

10 Skim any excess fat from the cooking liquid, taste, and reseason if needed.

11 Slice the brisket against the grain on the bias. Serve drizzled with the sauce and sprinkled with chives.

a tisket, a tasket – a brisket in my belly!

grilled hanger steak
with bagna cauda sauce

SERVES 2 TO 4 TIME ABOUT 2½ HOURS, LARGELY UNATTENDED

Some people go crazy for hanger steak. I'm one of those people who really loves it—especially when you dress it up with a hot bath of beautiful bagna cauda sauce, a northern Italian classic. This recipe is really about the sauce—a super-sexy, yummy anchovy-garlic butter. This sauce works on hanger steak or whatever cut floats your boat. Just give the meat a big fat drizzle of the hot bath and, once again, the little fish that people think they don't like ends up stealing the show!

MISE EN PLACE

FOR THE HANGER STEAK

2 cloves garlic, smashed and finely chopped

4 sprigs of fresh thyme, leaves chopped

Pinch of crushed red pepper

Extra virgin olive oil

2 hanger steaks, 1 to 2 pounds, trimmed

Kosher salt

FOR THE BAGNA CAUDA

5 anchovy fillets, oil-packed and drained

4 cloves garlic, smashed

2 sprigs of fresh thyme

Pinch of crushed red pepper

3 tablespoons extra virgin olive oil

Juice of ½ lemon

6 tablespoons unsalted butter, cut into pats

FOR THE STEAK

1   In a dish large enough to hold the steaks, combine the garlic, thyme, and crushed red pepper. Whisk in enough olive oil to make a loose paste.

2   Season the steaks generously with salt and add them to the dish with the garlic mixture. Coat the steaks completely and let sit at room temperature for 2 hours (if marinating for longer than 2 hours, toss them in the fridge).

3   Preheat a grill or cast-iron frying pan to medium-high heat (if using a cast-iron pan, coat it lightly with olive oil before heating).

4   Grill or sear the steaks for 4 to 5 minutes on each side. Transfer the steaks to a cutting board and let rest for 8 to 10 minutes before slicing.

(recipe continues)

FOR THE BAGNA CAUDA

1   In a small sauté pan, combine the anchovies, garlic, thyme, and crushed red pepper with the olive oil, then turn the heat to low. Cook, whisking occasionally, until the anchovies have dissolved and the garlic is roasty, 8 to 10 minutes.

2   Remove the thyme sprigs and whisk in the lemon juice. (NOTE: If you're not ready to use the sauce immediately, stop here, turn off the heat, and pick it up when you are ready to serve.)

3   Bring the pan to medium heat. Whisk in the butter, one pat at a time, waiting until each pat has almost melted before adding the next.

4   To serve, slice the steak against the grain into 1/2-inch-thick slices and drizzle with the sauce.

hang on – that's good!

shepherd's pie

SERVES **4 TO 6** TIME **ABOUT 2 HOURS**

I'm crazy for shepherd's pie. Put a mashed potato on top of any kind of stew and I'm a happy, happy girl. Call it shepherd's pie, fisherman's pie, or fireman's pie—call it any kind of pie, I love it. My only problem is that after years of working in restaurant kitchens and only having time to eat once the food was already cold, I just can't taste food when it's really hot anymore! With this pie, that top layer of mash acts like insulation, keeping the meat and veggies screaming hot. And because I'm impatient, I always dig in right away and I always burn my mouth. That sucks, but the good part is that whenever I make this for my Irish friends, they're always super happy and they bring the drinks—and that rocks!

MISE EN PLACE

FOR THE LAMB STEW

Extra virgin olive oil

2 pounds boneless lamb shoulder or leg, cut into 1/2-inch dice

Kosher salt

1/2 cup all-purpose flour

4 leeks, white parts only, cut into 1/2-inch dice

3 celery ribs, cut into 1/4-inch dice

3 carrots, cut into 1/4-inch dice

2 cloves garlic, smashed and finely chopped

1/4 cup tomato paste

1 cup Guinness stout

3 cups chicken stock

2 bay leaves

1 thyme bundle

1 cup frozen peas

FOR THE PIE

2 pounds Yukon gold potatoes, peeled and cut into 1-inch dice

Kosher salt

1 cup heavy cream

3 tablespoons unsalted butter

TO MAKE THE LAMB STEW

1   Coat a large, wide pan with olive oil and bring to medium-high heat.

2   Season the lamb with salt and toss with the flour. Working in batches, add half the lamb to the pan and brown well on all sides, 8 to 10 minutes total. Remove from the pan and repeat with the remaining lamb.

3   Ditch the oil from the pan and add a splash of fresh oil. Add the leeks, celery, and carrots to the pan, season with salt, and cook over medium heat until the veggies are soft and aromatic, 7 to 8 minutes. Toss in the garlic and cook for 1 to 2 more minutes.

(recipe continues)

4   Add the lamb and tomato paste and stir to combine. Cook until the tomato paste starts to brown, 2 to 3 minutes.

5   Add the Guinness and cook until the liquid has evaporated by half. Then add enough stock to just cover the lamb. Toss in the bay leaves and thyme bundle. Taste and season with salt if needed—it will be.

6   Bring the liquid to a boil and reduce to a simmer (BTB, RTS). Partially cover the pan and cook the stew, stirring occasionally, for 1 hour or until the lamb is tender. If the cooking liquid reduces, add a little more stock to keep the lamb just about covered.

7   When the lamb is tender, remove the lid to allow the liquid to cook down and thicken until it reaches a stew-like consistency. Taste and adjust the seasoning if needed.

8   Remove the thyme bundle and the bay leaves and discard. Stir in the frozen peas and remove from the heat.

TO MAKE THE PIE

1   Place the potatoes in a large saucepan with water to cover by 1 inch. Salt the water generously and bring it to a boil (BTB). Boil the potatoes until fork-tender, 15 to 20 minutes.

2   Drain the potatoes. While they're still hot, pass through a food mill into a large bowl and reserve.

3   In a small saucepan bring the cream to a boil.

4   Add half the butter and half the hot cream to the potatoes and whip until combined. Add the remaining butter and cream and repeat the process. Taste and season if needed. The potatoes should be very creamy and flavorful.

5   Preheat the broiler.

6   Transfer the lamb stew to a wide, flat baking dish. Spread the potatoes over the lamb stew in an even layer. Use the back of a spoon to create lots of peaks and valleys in the mashed potatoes—these will brown nicely under the broiler. (If you wanna get fancy, use a pastry bag outfitted with a large star tip to pipe the potatoes onto the stew.)

7   Put the whole shootin' match under the broiler until the potatoes are brown and crispy, 4 to 5 minutes. Serve immediately.

i'll be the shepherd of THAT pie!!

hawaiian pork roast

SERVES 6 TO 8   TIME ABOUT 2 DAYS, LARGELY UNATTENDED

When I was in Hawaii I was invited to a luau, a traditional event where a whole pig is buried and then cooked for twenty-four hours. I was SOOOOO excited to try this famous pork dish. But I was totally disappointed—it was dry and flavorless. I've been trying to amend that memory and replace it with beautiful thoughts of the ocean, the sunset that night, and the sway of the hula dancers. I've also tried to replace my recollections of that dinner by coming up with my own Hawaiian-style roast pork that is absolutely delicious. So start planning your luau-themed dinner party now!

MISE EN PLACE

5 cloves garlic, smashed and finely chopped

2-inch piece of fresh ginger, peeled and grated

1/2 cup rice wine vinegar

1/2 cup soy sauce

1 cup pineapple juice

1 cup oyster sauce

Grated zest and juice of 1 orange

3 star anise

1/4 cup packed dark or light brown sugar

2 tablespoons sambal oelek or Asian chili paste

1 5- to 5 1/2-pound bone-in pork roast with 6 rib bones

Extra virgin olive oil

ANNE ALERT For the best results, plan ahead and marinate the pork for 24 to 48 hours.

1   In a wide, flat dish large enough to accommodate the pork, combine the garlic, ginger, vinegar, soy sauce, pineapple juice, oyster sauce, orange zest and juice, star anise, brown sugar, and sambal. Stir to combine. Lay the pork, meaty side down, in the marinade and cover with plastic wrap. Refrigerate for 24 to 48 hours, turning over periodically.

2   Preheat the oven to 350°F.

3   Remove the pork from the marinade and let it come to room temperature.

4   Transfer the marinade to a medium saucepan, bring to a boil, and reduce to a simmer (BTB, RTS). Cook the marinade until it thickens to a brushable consistency, sort of like barbecue sauce, about 10 minutes.

5   Coat a large, wide, shallow pan with olive oil and bring to medium-high heat. Add the pork and brown it really well on all sides. This will take 10 to 15 minutes. Mmmmm . . . you know how I feel about *brown* food.

★ ★
(recipe continues) ★

6   Transfer the pork to a rimmed baking sheet outfitted with a rack. Brush the pork all over with the lovely sauce and transfer it to the oven. Carefully pour 1 cup water into the bottom of the pan (this will keep the sauce from burning as it drips off the meat).

7   Roast the pork for 15 minutes, brush generously with more sauce, turn the pork over, and return to the oven. By now the pork should be starting to get really crispy and sticky. Check to make sure there is still water in the bottom of the pan and add more if needed. Repeat this process in

15 minutes and then every 15 minutes for about 1½ hours, or until the internal temp registers 135°F. with an instant-read thermometer. If the outside of the pork starts to burn, tent it loosely with aluminum foil.

8   Remove the pork from the oven, cover loosely with aluminum foil (if it isn't already), and let rest for 20 minutes.

9   Cut the pork off the bone and into ½-inch slices. Transfer to a serving platter. Cut the ribs in between the bones and add to the serving platter. Serve the pork drizzled with any extra sauce.

now THAT'S a luau... aloha baby!

mustard-braised pork shoulder

SERVES 6 TO 8   TIME ABOUT 4 HOURS

The Italians always say when it comes to the pig you can use anything but the oink. Well, this is certainly true of pork shoulder—it's a blank canvas for your creative instincts. What you choose to do with it depends on how you're feeling that day. It's like a golden retriever—it gets along with everybody and everyone likes it. You can braise a shoulder, grind it to make sausage, use it in stuffing, even grill it. And it has a fantastic ratio of lean meat to fat, so it creates a great mouthfeel. The only thing you can't do with pork shoulder is be wishy-washy. You want to cook it either really fast or low and slow. My recipe is all about low and slooooowwwww . . .

MISE EN PLACE

1 4-pound boneless pork picnic shoulder

Kosher salt

Extra virgin olive oil

2 onions, cut into 2-inch chunks

3 celery ribs, cut into 1/2-inch dice

1 fennel bulb, cut into 1/2-inch dice

6 cloves garlic, smashed

2 cups dry white wine

1/2 teaspoon crushed red pepper

3 sprigs of fresh rosemary, leaves finely chopped

1/4 cup Dijon mustard

1/4 cup whole-grain mustard

3 to 4 cups chicken stock

3 bay leaves

1 thyme bundle

1 Preheat the oven to 375°F.

2 Season the pork generously with salt. Coat a Dutch oven with olive oil and bring to high heat. Add the pork and brown really well on all sides, 15 to 20 minutes total.

3 While the pork is browning, combine the onions, celery, fennel, and garlic in the bowl of a food processor and purée to a coarse paste.

4 When the pork is super brown, remove it from the pan and reserve. Ditch the fat in the pan and add some fresh oil. Add the puréed veggies, season with salt, and cook over medium heat until nicely browned, another 10 to 12 minutes.

5 Add the wine, crushed red pepper, and rosemary and cook until the wine has evaporated by half. Stir in the Dijon and whole-grain mustards. Add 2 cups of the chicken stock, taste, and season with salt if needed.

6   Return the pork to the pan and toss in the bay leaves and thyme bundle. The liquid level in the pan should come halfway up the sides of the pork. If needed, add more stock. If it's a bit high, don't worry about it. Put the lid on the Dutch oven and place it in the oven.

7   Braise the pork for 1 hour, turn it over, cover, and cook for 1 more hour. Add more liquid if needed.

8   Turn the pork over again and cook UNcovered for 45 minutes. At this point the braising liquid should begin to concentrate and become really flavorful.

9   Remove the pan from the oven, transfer the pork to a rimmed baking sheet, and loosely tent it with aluminum foil. Let the pork rest for 20 minutes. Skim any excess fat off the surface of the cooking liquid and place the pan over medium-high heat to reduce to your desired consistency. Fish out the bay leaves and thyme bundle.

10 Slice the pork and serve with the braising liquid.

this is no cold shoulder !!

rack of lamb
with harissa

Mmmmm . . . Middle Eastern spices. Every time I think about these exotic flavors my mouth just starts to water. I was first introduced to harissa by Mario Batali during an *Iron Chef* battle. He helped open up the world of flavors and spices to me and showed me that it's not all about Italian ALL the time. The heat of harissa—which is a North African chili sauce—is made for the luscious flavor of lamb. Sure, lamb is already yummy, but when you accent it with the deliciousness of this spice paste, it's like putting makeup on a beautiful woman—it just enhances the whole thing. There are lots of commercial versions of harissa, but it's easy to make it yourself, and in my opinion, way better. Whether you use it on this lovely little rack of lamb, add it to a stew, or toss it in a pita, it's a super secret-flavor weapon from the Mediterranean I'm sure you'll be happy to become acquainted with.

MISE EN PLACE

FOR THE LAMB

2 8-rib racks of lamb, Frenched

Kosher salt

Extra virgin olive oil

FOR THE HARISSA

2 red bell peppers

2 teaspoons cumin seed, toasted and ground

2 teaspoons coriander seed, toasted and ground

2 teaspoons fennel seed, toasted and ground

2 teaspoons caraway seed, toasted and ground

4 dried red chilies, coarsely chopped

3 cloves garlic, smashed and finely chopped

2 tablespoons red wine vinegar

¼ cup tomato paste

Kosher salt

½ cup extra virgin olive oil

ANNE-NOTATION To "French" a rack of lamb means you remove all the meat, fat, and membranes from between each of the ribs. It gives the racks a clean, elegant look, and your butcher is usually happy to do it for you.

TO PREPARE THE LAMB CHOPS

1   Remove 2 ribs from each rack to make it a 6-rib rack: Do this by starting from either end and removing the second and seventh bone. This creates six chops that are thicker than a normal lamb chop—YUM!!

2   Cut each rack into 6 equal chops, place on a baking sheet, and transfer to the fridge.

TO MAKE THE HARISSA

1 Preheat a grill.

2 Place the bell peppers on the grill and cook them on all sides until the skin is black and charred. Transfer the peppers to a large bowl, cover with plastic wrap, and let them hang out until cool. **HINT, HINT:** This can totally be done ahead! YAY!

3 Scrape the black charred skin off the peppers and remove the stem and seeds. Coarsely chop the peppers and transfer them to the bowl of a food processor.

4 Add the cumin, coriander, fennel, caraway, chilies, garlic, vinegar, and tomato paste to the food processor and season with salt. Purée until smooth.

5 Add $\frac{1}{4}$ cup of the olive oil to the mixture and pulse, pulse, pulse. Add the remaining $\frac{1}{4}$ cup olive oil and pulse again until thoroughly combined. Taste and season with salt. Taste again and reseason if needed. Store in an airtight container until ready to use.

TO MAKE THE LAMB

1 Preheat the oven to 250°F. Remove the lamb from the fridge, season generously with salt, and let sit for 15 to 20 minutes before cooking.

2 Coat a large sauté pan with olive oil and bring the pan to medium-high heat. Working in batches to avoid crowding the pan, add the lamb chops and cook for 3 to 4 minutes on each side for medium-rare (if you like your meat a little more well done, lower the heat and cook them a minute or two longer). If the pan begins to smoke, lower the heat. The chops will be beautifully browned on each side. Stand up the chops to brown the fat edge along each chop. YUM!!! Brown food tastes good!

3 Place the cooked chops on a baking sheet and transfer to the oven to keep them hot while the others cook.

4 Top each lamb chop with a spoonful of harissa and serve.

annie had a little lamb (chop)!!

pork porterhouse
with apple, prune, and saba sauce

SERVES 4 TO 6 TIME ABOUT 1½ HOURS, PLUS 24 HOURS OF BRINING

Everyone likes chops and applesauce. My version is a sophisticated, sexy take on this traditional dish. I think originally people paired pork chops with apple-sauce because the chops were super thin, dry, and had no flavor. The applesauce was there for moisture. Now that we have beautiful artisanal pork and so many amazing varieties of apples, I've taken what was formerly known as dry chops and jarred sauce and made it something super special—especially with the addition of the saba or vincotta, which is grape juice that's been reduced (and which would typically be used to make balsamic vinegar or wine). You'll find the flavor is bright and delicious—similar to balsamic but without the acid.

MISE EN PLACE

FOR THE BRINE

2 tablespoons kosher salt

1 tablespoon sugar

3 cloves garlic, smashed

3 sprigs of fresh rosemary

2 bay leaves

2 22- to 24-ounce pork porterhouse steaks

Extra virgin olive oil

FOR THE SAUCE

2 slices bacon, cut into lardons

Extra virgin olive oil

1 small onion, cut into ¼-inch dice

Kosher salt

2 Granny Smith apples, peeled and cut into ½-inch dice

1 cup prunes, quartered

2 sprigs of fresh rosemary, leaves finely chopped

¾ cup saba or vincotto

¾ cup chicken stock

2 tablespoons red wine vinegar

ANNE ALERT This is definitely a "think ahead" recipe—unless you decide not to brine the chops, which is NOT recommended!

TO BRINE THE PORK

1 In a container large enough to hold the pork and the brine, combine the salt, sugar, garlic, rosemary, bay leaves, and 2 quarts water. Stir to combine and add the pork. Cover and toss the whole shootin' match in the fridge for 24 hours.

2 When ready to cook, remove the chops and discard the brine. Let the pork come to room temp for 15 to 20 minutes, then pat dry and rub lightly with olive oil.

(recipe continues)

FOR THE SAUCE

1   Place the bacon in a large, straight-sided sauté pan along with a few drops of olive oil. Bring the pan to medium heat and cook until the bacon is brown and crispy, 6 to 7 minutes.

2   Add the onion and season with salt. Continue to cook until soft and very aromatic, 5 to 6 minutes.

3   Toss in the apples, prunes, and rosemary and cook for 3 to 4 minutes.

4   Stir in the saba, chicken stock, and vinegar. Bring to a boil, then reduce to a simmer (BTB, RTS) and cook for 15 to 20 minutes, or until the mixture has thickened to a saucy consistency. Taste and adjust the seasoning if needed.

TO COOK THE PORK

1   Preheat a grill to medium.

2   Grill the pork for 9 to 10 minutes on each side and then for an additional 1 to 2 minutes with the meat standing up on the fat edge to get it really crispy—YUM!

3   Remove the pork from the grill, transfer to a platter or cutting board, and cover loosely with foil. Let the pork rest for 12 to 15 minutes. To serve, cut each steak off the bone, slice thinly on the bias, and drizzle with sauce. Be sure to serve the bones as well in case anyone is feeling animal and wants to chew on them.

i want to live in this house!!!

braised pork belly

with cumin and ginger

SERVES 6 TO 8 TIME ABOUT 7 HOURS, PLUS OVERNIGHT MARINATING

I am seeing pork belly on so many restaurant menus. I'm almost pork-bellied out, but since I am still on the pork belly wagon, I came up with this recipe that integrates warm spices into the mix. Now, I know that most people think of pork belly as restaurant food, but if you've never made it yourself, it's worth doing. There's something very satisfying about being able to create a dish like this in your own kitchen—and you can!

MISE EN PLACE

FOR THE DRY RUB

2 tablespoons kosher salt

2 tablespoons cumin seed, toasted and finely ground

2 tablespoons coriander seed, toasted and finely ground

2 tablespoons ground ginger

2 tablespoons packed light or dark brown sugar

Grated zest of 1 lemon

2 cloves garlic, smashed and finely chopped

½ teaspoon crushed red pepper

4 pounds pork belly, skin removed

FOR THE BRAISE

Extra virgin olive oil

2 onions, julienned

3 celery ribs, sliced thinly on the bias

½ fennel bulb, julienned

Kosher salt

Pinch of crushed red pepper

3 cloves garlic, smashed and finely chopped

2-inch piece of fresh ginger, peeled and grated

1 cup white wine

2 to 3 cups chicken stock

1 thyme bundle

2 bay leaves

ANNE ALERT Another plan-ahead! This dry rub is best when you let it sit for at least 24 hours.

FOR THE DRY RUB

1   In a small bowl, combine the salt, cumin, coriander, ginger, brown sugar, lemon zest, garlic, and crushed red pepper.

2   Massage the dry rub all over the pork belly. Cover and refrigerate for 24 hours.

TO BRAISE THE PORK

1   Preheat the oven to 325°F.

2   Remove the pork belly from the fridge and let it come to room temperature.

(recipe continues)

3   Coat a large, wide, straight-sided ovenproof pan with olive oil. Add the onions, celery, and fennel to the pan and bring to medium-high heat. Season with salt and crushed red pepper, and cook the veggies until soft and very aromatic, 8 to 10 minutes. Toss in the garlic and ginger and cook for another 2 to 3 minutes.

4   Add the wine and cook until reduced by half, about 4 minutes. Add 2 cups chicken stock, the thyme bundle, and the bay leaves. Taste and reseason if needed . . . it will be.

5   NESTLE the pork belly into the pan. The liquid should come half to two-thirds of the way up the pork belly. Cover and place in the oven. Braise the pork belly for 6 hours, checking and rotating the pan every hour or so. If the liquid reduces too much, add the remaining stock as needed.

6   When the pork is done it will be very tender and succulent. Remove the lid and set the oven to broil. Broil, keeping a close eye on it, until the pork is golden brown and crispy, 3 to 4 minutes.

7   Remove the belly from the braising liquid and reserve on a rimmed baking sheet. Skim off the excess fat and reduce the braising liquid if needed. Discard the thyme and bay. Taste to make sure it is delicious and reseason if needed.

8   Divide the pork belly and serve with the reduced braising liquid.

I LOVE a tender belly!

girl chef's grilled lobster

SERVES 4 TIME **ABOUT 1 HOUR**

People always think of lobster as something you order at a fancy restaurant. Then you sit there, all decked out, and you have to wear a bib! That is just NOT for me. I'd rather be at a picnic table with an ice-cold beer in hand, not worried about getting dirty. I love that summer feeling of bare feet, slightly sunburned skin, and the taste of sweet lobster. I just peel off my splattered T-shirt and hose down. This lobster is pretty special—the claws are cracked and the body is split in half and stuffed with shrimp, corn, and cherry tomatoes.

MISE EN PLACE

1 pound 16-20 count shrimp, peeled and deveined

2 cloves garlic, smashed and finely chopped

Extra virgin olive oil

Kosher salt

1 lemon, halved

4 1¼- to 1½-pound lobsters

4 ears of corn, shucked

1 pint cherry tomatoes, halved

½ small red onion, thinly sliced

6 tablespoons red wine vinegar

5 fresh basil leaves, cut into a chiffonade

---

1. In a large bowl, toss the shrimp with the garlic, 2 tablespoons olive oil, and a generous sprinkle of salt. Let the shrimp sit at room temperature for 30 minutes.

2. Bring a large pot of well-salted water to a boil. Squeeze the juice from the lemon into the water and drop both halves into the pot.

3. Plunge the lobsters into the water, cover, and cook for 4 minutes. Carefully remove the lobsters from the water and let them cool. The lobsters will NOT be cooked through at this point.

4. Preheat a grill to medium.

5. Cover half the grill with 2 layers of aluminum foil and place the shrimp in a single layer on the foil (this will prevent the shrimp from falling through the grates). Grill the shrimp on both sides until pink and opaque, 2 to 3 minutes per side. Remove the shrimp and transfer to a large bowl.

6. While the shrimp are cooking, use the other half of the grill to cook the corn until charred on all sides, about 10 minutes. Remove the corn and let cool. Cut the corn off the cob and add it to the bowl with the shrimp. Holding the corn vertically on your cutting board, run your knife up the cobs to get the lovely little remnants

(recipe continues)

of the corn kernels and add these to the bowl as well. Be sure to get these bits—they are sweet and delicious and not to be missed!

7   Toss the cherry tomatoes and onion with the shrimp and corn. Add the vinegar and a few drops of olive oil. Stir to combine and season with salt. Taste and reseason if needed.

8   Twist the claws off the lobsters. Using a large, very sharp knife, cut the lobster bodies in half lengthwise. Commit to this—you can do it! Remove the contents of the cavity and discard. Save the tomalley (the green stuff) and the coral (the red stuff) for another purpose if desired.

9   Place the lobsters cut side down on the grill along with the claws. Grill the lobsters for 10 minutes and the claws for 15 minutes, being sure to turn the claws halfway through cooking.

10 Transfer the lobsters to serving plates—2 halves, cut side up, and 2 claws per plate. To serve, add the basil to the shrimp-corn mixture and spoon it into the cavity of each lobster.

aaaahhh ... hello summer.

crispy skate
in "crazy water"

SERVES 4   TIME ABOUT 1 HOUR

In Italian, "crazy water" is called *acqua pazza*. One of the stories I've heard is that fishermen used to make this dish using straight seawater, and it got its name because the water was so crazy salty. I don't think that's true. But it is yummy. Skate is the wing of a ray, and it's great because it's cheap to buy, fast to cook, and incredibly delicious. You get a bit of everything with this dish: it's crispy, juicy, and tender. And the lovely part is, the crazy water can be made ahead—isn't that just CRAZY???

MISE EN PLACE

FOR THE CRAZY WATER

Extra virgin olive oil

1 onion, coarsely chopped

1 celery rib, coarsely chopped

1/2 fennel bulb, coarsely chopped

Kosher salt

6 cloves garlic

1 pound fish bones, from cod or other white fish

3/4 cup dry white wine

1 lemon, halved

1 thyme bundle

1 bay leaf

FOR THE FISH

Extra virgin olive oil

3 fingerling potatoes, sliced into rounds

1 onion, julienned

1/2 fennel bulb, julienned

Kosher salt

2 cloves garlic, smashed and finely chopped

1 zucchini, green part only (discard the starchy, seedy part), julienned

12 grape tomatoes, halved lengthwise

Pinch of crushed red pepper

1 cup dry white wine

4 6- to 8-ounce skate wings

1 tablespoon fennel seed, toasted and finely ground

1 cup all-purpose flour

ANNE-NOTATION You can buy fish bones from your fishmonger, or you can buy a whole fish, cook it, and save the bones to use in this dish!

FOR THE CRAZY WATER

1   Coat a large pot lightly with olive oil. Toss in the onion, celery, and fennel and bring the pan to medium-high heat. Season the veggies with salt and cook until soft and very aromatic, 7 to 8 minutes. Add the garlic and cook for another 2 to 3 minutes.

2   Add the fish bones and wine, stir to combine, and cook until the wine has evaporated by half, 4 to 5 minutes.

(recipe continues)

3   Add 2 quarts water to the pan. Squeeze the juice from both halves of the lemon into the pot and drop them in. Toss in the thyme bundle and bay leaf. Bring the liquid to a boil, reduce to a simmer (BTB, RTS), and cook for 20 minutes. Taste and season the crazy water with salt as needed.

4   Strain the veggies and bones from the liquid and discard, reserving the crazy water until ready to use. **HINT, HINT:** All this can SO be done ahead!!!

FOR THE FISH

1   Coat a large, straight-sided sauté pan with olive oil. Add the potato rounds to the pan and brown on both sides, 4 to 5 minutes total. Remove from the pan and reserve.

2   Ditch the fat from the pan, add a few drops of fresh oil, and bring the pan to medium-high heat. Add the onion and fennel and season with salt. Cook until the veggies begin to soften, 4 to 5 minutes. Toss in the garlic, zucchini, tomatoes, and crushed red pepper and cook for 2 to 3 minutes.

3   Add the white wine and cook for 4 to 5 more minutes.

4   Add the crazy water to the pan until it covers the veggies by about $1/2$ inch. Simmer the whole story for 10 to 15 minutes, then taste to make sure it is delicious.

5   While the veggies cook, coat a large sauté pan with olive oil and bring to high heat.

6   Season the skate with salt and the ground fennel seed. Dust the fish in flour and spank off the excess. Place it IMMEDIATELY in the hot oil—NO PAUSING between the flour and the oil!!! Work in batches if your pan is not large enough to accommodate all the skate at one time.

7   Cook the fish on both sides until golden brown and crispy, 2 to 3 minutes per side. Remove the fish from the pan and blot on paper towels. Transfer to a platter.

8   Using a slotted spoon, strain the veggies from the crazy water and make a tall pile of them in the center of 4 soup bowls.

9   To serve, gently place a skate fillet on the top of each veg pile and ladle some of the crazy water into the bottom of each bowl.

that's just crazy!

fish and chips

SERVES **4 TO 6** TIME **ABOUT 45 MINUTES**

Who doesn't like fried fish? In Cazenovia, New York, where I'm from, Thursday night was always fish-fry night at Albert's, our local joint. And it was always haddock. Then when I went to London, many years later, the first meal I had was fish and chips. I got off the plane and went directly to a pub and ordered it. It was made with cod, and honestly, to me it's not about the kind of fish, it's about the batter! What you want in great fried fish is a really crispy, crunchy, light coating. Add to that some fabulous French fries and malt vinegar, and, hello? Do I really need to say more?

MISE EN PLACE

FOR THE TARTAR SAUCE

2 large egg yolks

1/4 cup malt vinegar

1 1/2 cups peanut oil

2 shallots, finely diced

3/4 cup finely chopped cornichons

1/2 cup whole-grain mustard

1 teaspoon celery salt, or more to taste

Pinch of cayenne pepper

FOR THE CHIPS

3 quarts peanut or other neutral-flavored oil for frying

4 large russet potatoes, peeled and cut lengthwise into 3/4-inch-wide sticks (hold the sticks in water until ready to use)

Kosher salt

FOR THE FISH

1 1/2 cups all-purpose flour, plus more if needed

1 tablespoon Old Bay seasoning

1 1/2 teaspoons baking soda

Kosher salt

1 12-ounce bottle ice-cold beer or sparkling water, plus more if needed

2 pounds cod, haddock, or grouper fillets, skinned and cut diagonally into 1 1/2-inch wide strips, about 5 inches long

ANNE-NOTATION A deep-fry thermometer will ensure great fried food every time.

FOR THE TARTAR SAUCE

1   In a food processor, combine the egg yolks and malt vinegar.

2   With the machine running, add the oil a drop at a time until the mixture starts to look homogeneous, thick, and silky. When the mixture has thickened, you can add the oil a little bit faster until all the oil has been incorporated.

(recipe continues)

3   Add the shallots, cornichons, mustard, celery salt, and cayenne. Pulse the machine a couple times to combine everything. Taste and adjust the seasoning with a little more celery salt if needed. Reserve until ready to use.

FOR THE CHIPS

1   Place the oil in a wide, deep pot and bring it to 325°F. as measured by a deep-fry thermometer.

2   Remove the potatoes from the water and pat dry. (Don't skip the drying—or they'll splatter when they hit the oil and burn you!)

3   Set up your drying situation by the stove—line a baking sheet with several layers of paper towels.

4   Working in batches, fry the potatoes until they are cooked through but have very little color, 6 to 7 minutes.

5   Use a slotted spoon to transfer the potatoes to the prepared baking sheet and continue cooking until all the potatoes are done.

6   Crank up the heat on the oil and bring it to 375°F. Working in batches again, fry the potatoes a second time to make them really golden brown and crispy, another 5 to 6 minutes. Remove the fries from the oil, place on the paper towels, and sprinkle immediately with salt. Try not to eat them all right away! (NOTE: This step can also be done AFTER the fish is fried. Just be sure to keep the fish warm in a 200°F. oven.)

FOR THE FISH

1   Preheat the oven to 200°F. Heat the oil to 375°F. and set up a baking sheet lined with several layers of paper towels. Set up another baking sheet with a baking rack.

2   In a medium bowl, combine the flour, Old Bay, baking soda, and a couple pinches of salt. Make a well in the center of the flour mixture and gently stir in the beer. Mix until JUST combined. If the batter seems too thick, add a bit more beer. If it seems too thin, add a bit more flour. Dip the fish fillets in the batter to generously coat them.

3   Working in batches, add the fish to the hot oil: Hold the fish by one end and dip about half of the fish into the oil until the batter starts to puff up and float, then gently slide the fish the rest of the way into the oil. Fry the fish until golden brown and puffy, turning the pieces halfway through the cooking process, 5 to 6 minutes total.

4   When the fish is done, remove it from the oil, blot it dry on the paper towels, and sprinkle immediately with salt. Transfer the fish to the baking sheet with the rack and hold it in the oven. Repeat until all the fish is fried. Serve HOT with the chips and tartar sauce.

this fish didn't get away!!!.

seared wild striped bass

with fennel, pink grapefruit, and dandelion

SERVES 4 TIME ABOUT 45 MINUTES

When I was a kid, even in the dead of winter we would shovel a path outside so we could throw a fish on the grill. Then we would come in from the icy air, take off our coats, warm up, and have a smoky, crispy, tender fish with a refreshing salad of bitter greens—it was enough to make me forget I was hoping for a snow day! To make life a bit easier for those of you in snowy regions, I've tweaked this recipe so you can sear the fish inside and still get that yummy combo of flavors—all year round!

MISE EN PLACE

4 6-ounce wild striped bass fillets, skin on

Extra virgin olive oil

Kosher salt

2 cloves garlic, smashed

Pinch of crushed red pepper

1 fennel bulb, shaved on a mandoline

2 pink grapefruit, supremed over a bowl to catch all the juices

1 bunch dandelion greens, cut crosswise into 1-inch ribbons

½ small red onion, thinly sliced

Big fat finishing oil

1 Pat the skin of the fish dry with a paper towel and let it sit out for 15 to 20 minutes to come to room temperature.

2 Coat a large sauté pan generously with olive oil and bring it to high heat. While the pan is heating up, coat the bottom of a smaller sauté pan lightly with olive oil and set it aside—CLEARLY upside down!

3 Preheat the oven to 250°F.

4 Season the fish generously with salt. Place the fish skin side down in the heated pan and immediately place the smaller sauté pan directly on top of the fish. Gently press it down.

This will keep the fish skin directly in contact with the pan so it will get really crispy. REMEMBER to oil the bottom of the second pan or the fish will stick to it. Let the fish cook this way for 2 to 3 minutes. If the oil is smoking, turn down the heat to medium. Cook the fish for another 2 to 3 minutes. Transfer the fish from the sauté pan to a baking sheet and place in the oven. You want the fish cooked through but not dry.

5 Ditch the oil from the pan, coat the pan with fresh oil, and add the garlic and crushed red pepper. Over medium heat, cook the garlic until

(recipe continues)

it is golden and very aromatic, 2 to 3 minutes. Remove and discard the garlic—it has fulfilled its garlic destiny. Thank YOU for coming!

6   Add the fennel to the pan and season with salt. Continue cooking until it begins to soften and wilt. Add the juice from the grapefruit and turn off the heat.

7   Add the grapefruit supremes, dandelion greens, and red onion. Toss to combine and season with more salt as needed. Taste to make sure it is delicious.

8   To serve, place a mound of the fennel mixture in the center of each serving plate. Nestle a fish fillet into each mound and spoon any of the excess juice over each piece of fish. Drizzle each plate with a few drops of big fat finishing oil.

please pass the bass!

whole roasted fish
in salt crust

SERVES 2 TIME ABOUT 1 HOUR

This recipe looks so impressive and is so easy it's almost not fair. Get a whole fish (it's great if you've just been fishing and have hooked this), toss some herbs in the belly, mix salt with some egg whites, and toss it in the oven. You get the fun of cracking the salt crust off the fish at the table and then offering up a perfectly seasoned, juicy, succulent fish. You won't have to go fishing for compliments.

MISE EN PLACE

2 lemons, 1 zested and juiced, 1 sliced

1 bunch of fresh thyme, leaves from half, remaining sprigs left whole

3 fresh bay leaves, coarsely chopped

2 cloves garlic, smashed

6 large egg whites

5 cups kosher salt

1 3-pound whole fish, such as snapper, branzino, or orata (sea bream)

Big fat finishing oil

1   Preheat the oven to 450°F.

2   In the food processor, combine the lemon zest and juice, thyme leaves, bay leaves, and garlic. PULSE, pulse, pulse until a coarse paste forms.

3   Add the egg whites to the mixture and process until very frothy and foamy.

4   In a large bowl, combine the herb-egg mixture with the salt and stir to create a moist paste.

5   Spoon a little less than half the salt mixture onto a rimmed baking sheet and pat it into a long oval, a little bigger than the fish.

6   Lay the fish on the salt pedestal and fill the cavity of the fish with the lemon slices and the thyme sprigs.

Pack the remaining salt mixture firmly around the fish to completely encase it and create a crust.

7   Transfer the fish to the oven and roast for 25 minutes.

8   Remove the fish and let it rest for 10 minutes. Crack open the salt crust, remove the top layer, and brush the excess salt from the fish with a dry pastry brush.

9   Remove the top fillet of the fish and carefully transfer to a serving plate. Pull out the spine and discard. Transfer the bottom fillet to the serving plate as well and drizzle with big fat finishing oil to serve.

go fish!

olive oil–poached salmon
with kumquat compote

SERVES **4** TIME **ABOUT 1 HOUR**

Try saying kumquat compote five times fast! It's not easy. But whipping up this incredibly succulent dish is. You just cook the salmon in an olive oil bath (doesn't that just sound relaxing?) until it's tender and delicious. Then you add in the sweet, tangy citrus flavor of a little kumquat, and you've got a super-sexy meal going on.

MISE EN PLACE

FOR THE KUMQUAT COMPOTE

1/2 pound kumquats, cut into thirds and seeded

1/2 cup sugar

1/2 cup orange marmalade

1-inch piece of fresh ginger, peeled and grated

1/4 teaspoon cinnamon

1/2 red jalapeño, minced

1/4 cup champagne vinegar

1 thyme bundle

Kosher salt

FOR THE SALMON

4 cups extra virgin olive oil

4 cloves garlic, smashed

Pinch of crushed red pepper

1 thyme bundle

Zest of 1 lemon, peeled off in wide strips with a veggie peeler

1 tablespoon coriander seed

2 bay leaves

4 6-ounce salmon fillets, at room temperature

Kosher salt

FOR THE COMPOTE

In a small saucepan, combine the kumquats, sugar, marmalade, ginger, cinnamon, jalapeño, vinegar, thyme, pinch of salt, and 3/4 cup water. Stir to combine and bring to a simmer over medium heat. Stir until the water evaporates and the mixture thickens slightly, 15 to 20 minutes.

TO POACH THE SALMON

1 In a large, straight-sided pan, combine the olive oil, garlic, crushed red pepper, thyme bundle, lemon zest, coriander seed, and bay leaves. Bring the pan to medium heat and let simmer for about 15 minutes. This will really infuse and perfume the olive oil—YUM!

2 Season the fish generously with salt and slide it gently into the hot oil bath. Let the fish poach for about 15 minutes.

3 Gently remove the fish from the oil and blot on a paper towel. Transfer the salmon to a serving dish and top with the kumquat compote.

hello my cutie little kumquat!!!

squid fideua
with aïoli

SERVES **6 TO 8** TIME **ABOUT 1½ HOURS**

This may be the best baked fish dish you've ever had—tender squid cooked with broken spaghetti and then topped with a little aïoli to create a dish of pure loveliness. It's kind of like pasta paella—crusty on the edges with bits of broken pasta that look like there's a little porcupine in your dish! It's cute and yummy! Toss in some tomatoes, chickpeas, and other spicy flavors and you'll be so happy.

MISE EN PLACE

Extra virgin olive oil

1 onion, cut into ¼-inch dice

Kosher salt

Pinch of crushed red pepper

2 cloves garlic, smashed and finely chopped

1 link (about 4 ounces) Spanish chorizo, cut into ¼-inch dice

½ cup dry white wine

1 28-ounce can plum tomatoes, passed through a food mill

Pinch of saffron

¾ pound fideo or angel hair pasta, broken into 1-inch lengths

1½ pounds calamari, cleaned, bodies cut into ¼-inch rings

1 cup canned chickpeas, drained and rinsed

¾ cup chicken stock, plus more as needed

Aïoli (page 40)

½ bunch fresh Italian parsley, leaves finely chopped

1 Coat a wide, straight-sided pan with olive oil, add the onion, and season with salt and crushed red pepper. Bring the pan to medium heat. Cook the onion until soft and very aromatic, 7 to 8 minutes. Toss in the garlic and cook for another 1 to 2 minutes.

2 Add the chorizo and cook for 3 to 4 minutes.

3 Add the wine and cook until reduced by about half, then stir in the tomatoes, saffron, and 1 cup water and season with salt. Taste the sauce

to make sure you're on the right track—it should start to taste good. Bring to a boil, reduce to a simmer (BTB, RTS), and cook for 25 to 30 minutes, stirring occasionally. You want the sauce to thicken up so the flavor really concentrates. Remove the sauce from the heat and let cool for 15 to 20 minutes. DO A LITTLE QC here—taste again and reseason if needed.

4 Preheat the oven to 400°F.

(recipe continues)

5   Coat a large sauté pan with olive oil and bring it to medium heat. Add the pasta and cook, turning frequently, until it's toasty and turning a little bit brown, 4 to 5 minutes. Remove from the heat and let cool.

6   Toss the toasted pasta into the sauce, add the calamari, chickpeas, and chicken stock, and stir to combine.

7   Transfer the whole mixture to an ovenproof baking dish or paella pan. Put the dish on a baking sheet and place it in the oven. After 15 minutes, stir the mixture from top to bottom. If it seems dry, add about $1/2$ cup more stock. Rotate the dish and bake for another 15 minutes. The casserole is done when the liquid is fully absorbed, the pasta is cooked through, and the top is a little crispy.

8   To serve, spoon dollops of the aïoli randomly on top of the pasta and sprinkle with the parsley.

what delicious squidness!

Cranberry-Walnut Scones with Whipped Honey Butter

brunch

Whenever anyone says to me, "Hey, let's

go to brunch," I have visions of a restorative Bloody Mary and all the deliciousness that brunch entails. I realize that going out to brunch means I'll have to get out of bed and emerge into the world on Sunday morning, that I'll probably have to stand in line to get a table, and that the staff will be either too cranky or too perky. (I remember what it was like to be a line cook during brunch—it wasn't delightful.) As much as I love the idea of brunch, I prefer to eat it at home.

What I've realized over the years is that I'm a huge fan of brunch *food*—just not at brunch time . . . afternoons work much better for me. I became a chef so I could do everything later. I go to sleep late, work late, stay up late, and eat breakfast late. To me the perfect time for brunch is between two and five p.m.! I LOOOOOVE brunch food—it's the ultimate hangover cure and the perfect mix of salty, greasy comfort food.

There are a few different schools of thought when it comes to brunch, and most people fall decidedly into a specific camp. Are you a *sweet* brunch person who likes pancakes and French toast? Or are you a *savory* brunch person who likes big breakfast meat and eggs in any form? (Or are you a *fake savory* brunch person who orders egg white omelets with dry toast?) Are you a big, hearty, hair-of-the-dog brunch person, or are you a fruit and yogurt with a bowl of granola person? There are LOTS of different directions you can go with brunch, and while some people do like to mix it up, I myself am always a savory brunch girl—it's just how I roll.

I can make a mean pancake, but if you're asking me what I like to eat, I go the egg route, EVERY time. But I completely understand the sweet side, too. Some of my best friends are sweet brunch people, and there's nothing wrong with that! All of the dishes in this chapter are delicious for any meal—not strictly brunch. If you want to serve a beautiful baked egg as an appetizer or make a frittata for lunch, knock yourself out. REMEMBER: YOU ARE THE CHEF OF YOUR OWN KITCHEN, AND YOU CAN EAT WHATEVER, HOWEVER, AND, OF COURSE, WHENEVER YOU LIKE!

cranberry-walnut scones
with whipped honey butter

SERVES 8 TIME **ABOUT 1 HOUR**

I didn't grow up eating scones, but they are so quick and easy (Q&E) to make that I've come to love them—they always make brunch a little bit fancy, like a tea party! The beautiful thing about my scones is that they aren't the rock-hard kind. These are light, crumbly, and really tender. And once you make the dough, you can form them, freeze them, and then just whip them out and toss them in the oven for a quick warm treat. To make these even more special, I serve them with homemade honey butter—also super easy. We've all made butter before . . . by mistake. Sometimes you're making whipped cream and you think, "Just one or two more beats" and then, uh-oh! You've got butter. When I was a little kid, my mom would give me a jar with a pint of heavy cream in it and send me outside to shake the jar until I made butter. I thought it was so exciting. I was out in the sun and it would take FOREVER. I think my mom was just trying to get me out of her hair!

MISE EN PLACE

FOR THE SCONES

3 cups all-purpose flour, plus more as needed for dusting

1 cup granulated sugar

1 tablespoon baking powder

Zest of 1 orange

Pinch of kosher salt

12 tablespoons (1½ sticks) cold unsalted butter, cut into pea-size pieces

¾ cup heavy cream

1 cup dried cranberries

½ cup walnuts, coarsely chopped

Turbinado sugar

FOR THE HONEY BUTTER

1½ cups COLD heavy cream

¼ cup honey

FOR THE SCONES

1 Preheat the oven to 375°F. and line a baking sheet with parchment paper.

2 Place the flour, granulated sugar, baking powder, orange zest, and salt in the bowl of a food processor and pulse to combine. Add the butter and pulse, pulse, pulse until the mixture looks like crumbled Parmigiano

cheese, 20 to 30 seconds. Add the cream and continue pulsing until the mixture begins to come together in little balls about the size of gravel, being careful not to overwork the dough or it will become tough.

3 Turn the mixture onto a lightly floured work surface. Add the cranberries and walnuts and gently work them into

the dough. Don't knead the dough—just bring it together until it forms a homogeneous mixture, giving it a little tough love—be gentle, but firm.

4   Flatten the dough into a round disk about 1 inch thick. Cut the disk in half and then cut each half into 4 triangles. Place the dough triangles on the prepared baking sheet and sprinkle with a little turbinado sugar.

5   Bake for 16 to 18 minutes, or until golden on top.

super - sconeage!

1   Chill a metal mixing bowl in the freezer for 15 to 20 minutes. If you don't have a stand mixer, chill any bowl and use a hand mixer or a whisk to whip the cream. If using a whisk, chill it along with the bowl and use good old-fashioned elbow grease to whip your cream—it's a bit of work, but SOOOOO satisfying! (The cold part is important.)

2   Once the bowl has chilled, pour the COLD heavy cream into the bowl, add the honey, and beat until the cream begins to clump together, 7 to 8 minutes. Scrape the sides of the bowl and beat for another 1 to 2 minutes, or until the mixture is well combined. Use the butter right away or store in the fridge.

farro granola

SERVES 4 TO 6   TIME ABOUT 3 HOURS, MOSTLY UNATTENDED

I am a LOVER of the grain farro. But I am not typically a lover of granola—it's usually so hard I feel like I'm eating gravel. I know, it's supposed to be good for you, but next time you're crunching away on your bowl of "grains," check out the side of the package. Most granola is full of crap and really not that healthy at all. This granola is good for you and tastes yummy. The trick is to parboil the farro, dry it, toss it with some oil and honey, and then toast it. You get the incredible earthy flavor of the grain with a nice toothsome chew to it—no rocks included!

MISE EN PLACE

Kosher salt

2 tablespoons sugar

2 cups semipearled farro

2 tablespoons extra virgin olive oil

2 tablespoons honey

3/4 cup pepitas (green pumpkin seeds)

1/2 cup sliced almonds

1/2 cup shredded coconut

1/2 cup golden raisins

1/2 cup dried cranberries

1/2 cup dried apricots, quartered

ANNE-NOTATION The garnishes I suggest are optional, but totally delicious: Homemade Ricotta (page 163), diced apples or pears, more honey. And of course milk—whole milk, skim milk, soy milk, whatever you want!

1   Preheat the oven to 300°F.

2   Place a medium saucepan of water over high heat and bring to a boil (BTB). Season the water with salt and the sugar. Add the farro and let the water return to a boil. Cook for 5 to 6 minutes or until the farro is tender on the outside but still chewy on the inside. Drain the farro in a mesh strainer and spread it out on a baking sheet to cool.

3   When the farro is cool, put it in a large bowl and stir in the oil and honey. Mix to coat the farro thoroughly. Toss in the pepitas, almonds, and coconut and combine well.

4   Spread the farro mixture on a baking sheet and place in the oven for 15 minutes. Remove from the oven, stir, and bake for another 20 minutes or until golden. Remove from the oven, stir again, and let cool completely.

5   Once cooled, stir the granola and let it sit out on the baking sheet for at least 1 more hour, until completely dry. Add the raisins, cranberries, and apricots.

6   Eat immediately or store in an airtight container.

It's far-out!!

banana macadamia nut pancakes

with pineapple compote

SERVES 4   TIME **ABOUT 45 MINUTES**

Pancakes aren't usually how I roll. But when I was in Hawaii, I don't know if it was the jet lag or the sunshine, but I ordered these pancakes and totally loved them. And every time I think of these it takes me right back to Hawaii. I was sitting on my hotel balcony at the Halekulani in a plush hotel robe, looking out over Diamond Head and the glittery blue Pacific Ocean. Little birds were twirling around my head, singing good morning in their sweet little chirpy voices, and I was eating this delightful breakfast. It was one of those magical moments when I just stopped for a minute, put down my fork, and said to myself, "Going to culinary school got me here?" Who knew you could get *all that* from a pancake?

MISE EN PLACE

FOR THE PANCAKES

1½ cups all-purpose flour

¼ cup granulated sugar

2 teaspoons baking soda

Pinch of kosher salt

1½ cups buttermilk

2 tablespoons unsalted butter, melted, plus more as needed for cooking

2 large eggs

1 teaspoon vanilla extract

2 large ripe bananas, 1 puréed and 1 cut into ½-inch dice

¾ cup roasted macadamia nuts, coarsely chopped

Powdered sugar for dusting (optional)

FOR THE PINEAPPLE COMPOTE

½ cup packed light or dark brown sugar

1 cup spiced rum

2 vanilla beans, split and scraped

1 lemon, halved

1 pineapple, top, skin, and core removed, cut into bite-size pieces

FOR THE PANCAKES

1   Preheat the oven to 200°F.

2   In a large bowl, combine the flour, granulated sugar, baking soda, and salt.

3   In another large bowl, combine the buttermilk, melted butter, eggs, vanilla, and puréed banana and mix well.

4   Make a hole in the center of the dry ingredients and slowly pour in the

buttermilk mixture, stirring until JUST combined. Add the diced banana and macadamia nuts and mix gently to disperse.

5   Place a griddle over medium-high heat. When hot, drop a few pats of butter onto the griddle. Once melted, schmear the butter around and wipe up any excess with a paper towel.

6   Spoon ladlefuls of batter onto the buttered griddle—you can make them any size you like, big, small, whatever, just make them all the same size. Let the pancakes cook until bubbles appear on the surface, burst, and then stay open—this will take about 5 minutes. Flip the pancakes and cook the second side until golden brown. Re-butter the griddle and repeat until all the batter is gone or everyone is full. Hold the finished pancakes in the warm oven.

FOR THE COMPOTE

1   In a medium saucepan, combine the brown sugar, 1 1/2 cups water, rum, and vanilla beans and place over medium-high heat. Squeeze the juice from the lemon into the mixture and drop both halves into the pan. Bring the mixture to a boil and reduce to a simmer (BTB, RTS).

2   Toss in the pineapple and stir to combine. Continue to simmer until the liquid has reduced to a syrupy consistency and the pineapple is very tender, about 25 minutes. Fish out the lemon halves and drizzle the warm syrup over the pancakes. Dust with powdered sugar if desired.

aloha baby !!!

pumpkin-ricotta pancakes
with chunky apple-raisin sauce

SERVES 4 TIME **ABOUT 45 MINUTES**

As a kid, every now and then my mom would make pancakes for dinner—we called it backwards day, and I loved the idea of it. I prefer pancakes that are moist and light and delicious. The trick is to use ricotta cheese and egg whites to lighten the batter—then you'll get nice fluffy pancakes every time. Serve these with a batch of apple compote with some golden raisin action and you'll be a winner every time.

MISE EN PLACE

FOR THE PANCAKES

2 cups all-purpose flour

$3/4$ cup granulated sugar

1 heaping teaspoon baking powder

$1/2$ teaspoon cinnamon

Kosher salt

1 cup pumpkin purée (canned is okay!)

1 cup Homemade Ricotta (page 163) or store-bought

$3/4$ cup whole milk

1 teaspoon vanilla extract

4 large eggs, separated

Unsalted butter as needed

Powdered sugar (optional)

FOR THE COMPOTE

5 tablespoons unsalted butter

4 Granny Smith apples, peeled and cut into $1/2$-inch dice, and tossed with the juice of 1 lemon

$3/4$ cup apple cider

1 whole cinnamon stick

2 star anise

$1/4$ cup packed dark or light brown sugar

1 cup maple syrup

1 cup golden raisins

FOR THE PANCAKES

1 Preheat the oven to 200°F.

2 In a large bowl, combine the flour, granulated sugar, baking powder, cinnamon, and a pinch of salt. Make a hole in the center of the flour mixture and add the pumpkin, ricotta, milk, vanilla, and egg yolks and mix gently to combine.

3 In a medium bowl, combine the egg whites with a pinch of salt. Using a mixer or whisk, beat the egg whites until they hold stiff peaks and look very fluffy, like snowdrifts.

4 Using a rubber spatula, scoop a third of the egg whites into the pumpkin batter and fold to gently combine. Repeat this process two more times

(recipe continues)

piece of PAN-cake !!

until all the whites have been added. Do this gently but quickly—the idea is to not squish the air out of the egg whites. This is the secret to keeping the pancakes fluffy!

5   Place a griddle over medium-high heat. When the pan is hot, drop a pat or two of butter onto the griddle. Once melted, schmear the butter around and wipe up any excess with a paper towel.

6   Spoon ladlefuls of batter onto the buttered griddle to create 3-inch pancakes. Let the pancakes cook until bubbles appear on the surface, burst, and then stay open—this will take about 5 minutes. Flip the pancakes and cook the second side until golden brown. Re-butter the griddle and repeat until all the batter is gone or everyone is full. Hold the finished pancakes in the warm oven.

FOR THE COMPOTE

1   Melt the butter in a large saucepan over medium heat. Add the apples, cider, cinnamon stick, star anise, and brown sugar. Bring to a boil and reduce to a simmer (BTB, RTS), then continue cooking until the liquid has reduced by half.

2   Add the maple syrup and raisins. Simmer for another 3 to 4 minutes or until slightly thickened. Remove from the heat and serve spooned over the pancakes, dusted with powdered sugar if desired. Try not to eat too many.

zucchini quick bread

MAKES 2 LOAVES TIME ABOUT 1½ HOURS

Growing up, we had a vegetable garden and my mom always grew zucchini—we had zucchini coming out of our ears! And as is prone to happen with zucchini, some of them grew to be absolutely gigantic, so we made a lot of zucchini bread. Whenever I was going to someone's house my mom would say, "Take a loaf of zucchini bread." It was ridiculous. Once I left home, it took me a long time to want to make this lovely loaf again, let alone eat it, but now I love it as much as I did then. When I was writing this I reached out to my mother because I wanted to use the zucchini bread recipe I remember from growing up. And after all these years I found out it's not really her recipe; she got it from our across-the-street neighbor, Elli Weir! Who knew?

MISE EN PLACE

3 large eggs

2 cups sugar

1 cup vegetable oil, plus more for greasing the pans

Grated zest and juice of 1 lemon

2 cups grated zucchini

1 8-ounce can crushed pineapple, drained

3 cups all-purpose flour

2 teaspoons baking powder

1 teaspoon cinnamon

1 cup golden raisins

1 cup coarsely chopped walnuts

Pinch of salt

1 Preheat the oven to 350°F.

2 In a large mixing bowl, combine the eggs and sugar and beat with a hand mixer until foamy. Beat in the oil and lemon zest and juice.

3 Stir in the zucchini, pineapple, flour, baking powder, cinnamon, raisins, walnuts, and salt. Stir until well combined.

4 Grease 2 large loaf pans. Divide the batter between the pans. Bake for 1 hour, rotating the pans halfway through the cooking time. Remove from the oven and let cool before slicing.

ZUCH - YUMMIE!!

cherry blueberry turnovers

with cream cheese

MAKES 8 TIME **ABOUT 2 HOURS**

When I was a little kid, sometimes on Sunday mornings my mom would whip out a box of frozen turnovers, heat them up, and call that breakfast. It was such a treat! I still LOOOOOVE a good fruit turnover, but I haven't made puff pastry from scratch since I was in culinary school and it's a battle I choose not to fight (even restaurants buy frozen puff pastry). If you want to make your own, knock yourself out. You can spend your time making a really yummy filling instead and then getting back in bed to enjoy this special breakfast (maybe with someone else!).

MISE EN PLACE

1 cup blueberries, picked over and stems removed

1 cup pitted Bing cherries, halved

Grated zest and juice of $1/2$ lemon

6 tablespoons granulated sugar

$1/2$ 8-ounce package of cream cheese

$1/4$ teaspoon vanilla extract

2 tablespoons cornstarch

All-purpose flour as needed for dusting

2 sheets of frozen puff pastry, thawed in the fridge

2 large eggs, beaten with 2 tablespoons water

$3/4$ cup powdered sugar

FOR THE FILLING

1   In a large bowl, combine the blueberries, cherries, lemon zest and juice, and 2 tablespoons of the granulated sugar. Let the mixture sit at room temperature for 30 to 40 minutes.

2   In a medium bowl, combine the cream cheese, remaining $1/4$ cup sugar, and vanilla and let sit in the fridge for 30 minutes to firm up.

3   Transfer the fruit mixture to a small saucepan and bring the pan to medium heat.

4   While the fruit heats up, mix the cornstarch with 2 tablespoons water in a small bowl and stir until thoroughly combined (this is called a slurry). Add the slurry to the saucepan and continue to cook, stirring frequently, until the juices thicken, 4 to 5 minutes. Remove from the heat and let cool completely.

(recipe continues)

FOR THE PASTRY

Dust a work surface lightly with flour. Lay 1 puff pastry sheet on the floured surface, dust with a bit more flour, and roll it with a rolling pin to smooth and shape the dough into a square. Cut the puff pastry down the middle and across to create 4 equal squares. Place the squares on a baking sheet and place in the fridge. Repeat with the other pastry sheet.

TO ASSEMBLE THE TURNOVERS

1   Preheat the oven to 375°F. Line 2 baking sheets with parchment paper or silicone baking mats.

2   Remove the puff pastry squares from the fridge. Fold each pastry square in half diagonally to make a triangle, crimp gently along the folded edge to mark the middle, and then open back up again.

3   Place a dollop of the cream cheese filling below the crimp in the pastry. Repeat with all 8 squares, dividing the cream cheese equally.

4   Spoon the fruit filling over the cream cheese filling, being careful to keep the fruit on the bottom half of the square with the filling (and away from the edges of the pastry).

5   Brush the bottom edges of the pastry with some of the egg wash. Fold the top half of the pastry over to meet the bottom edge to form a perfect triangle. Crimp the edges shut with a fork. Brush the top of the pastry with more egg wash. Cut three $1/2$-inch slits in the top of each turnover to allow steam to escape and prevent blowouts. Repeat this process with the remaining pastry.

6   Place the turnovers on the lined baking sheets, leaving a generous amount of space between them. Transfer the turnovers to the oven and bake for 30 to 35 minutes, or until they are golden brown. Remove from the oven and let cool slightly.

7   While the turnovers bake, combine the powdered sugar with 2 tablespoons water. The mixture should have a drizzley, glazey consistency—add a little more water if necessary.

8   When the turnovers are cool enough to handle, drizzle them with the powdered sugar glaze and serve immediately.

turn OVER that's good!

french toast stuffed

with bacon, onion tomato jam with gruyère, and a fried egg

SERVES 4 TIME **ABOUT 1 HOUR**

When I make this dish people always say to me, "Who knew you could make savory French toast?" It's kind of like the breakfast version of grilled cheese, and it's the perfect combo of salty, sweet, cheesy, and delicious—in my opinion, it's the ultimate French toast. It's so versatile and so bursting with flavor that it can be breakfast, brunch, lunch, or dinner—and it will make you a rock star with your guests every time.

MISE EN PLACE

FOR THE FILLING

8 slices bacon, cut into 1/4-inch lardons

Extra virgin olive oil

1 onion, cut into 1/4-inch dice

Kosher salt

Pinch of crushed red pepper

1 large beefsteak tomato, seeded and cut into 1/2-inch dice

2 sprigs of fresh oregano, leaves finely chopped

FOR THE FRENCH TOAST

4 large eggs

1 cup whole milk

Pinch of cayenne (optional)

Kosher salt

8 slices tight-crumbed white bread

1 1/2 cups grated Gruyère cheese

FOR THE FRIED EGGS

Extra virgin olive oil

4 large eggs

1 bunch of fresh chives, finely chopped (optional)

FOR THE FILLING

1   Toss the bacon into a large sauté pan with a few drops of olive oil. Bring the pan to medium heat and cook the bacon until brown and crispy, 6 to 7 minutes. Add the onion and season with salt and the crushed red pepper. Continue to cook, stirring occasionally, until the onion is soft and very aromatic, 8 to 10 minutes.

2   Add the tomato, season with more salt, and cook for another 8 to 10 minutes or until the tomatoes are soft and mushy and most of the liquid has evaporated. Taste and reseason if needed. Stir in the oregano and let cool.

FOR THE FRENCH TOAST

1   Preheat the oven to 200°F.

2   In a wide, flat dish, combine the eggs, milk, cayenne (if using), and a pinch of salt. Beat until smooth and homogeneous.

(recipe continues)

3   Lay 4 slices of bread on a work surface. Using half the Gruyère, sprinkle each piece of bread lightly with cheese. Spoon a quarter of the bacon filling onto each piece of bread and then sprinkle with the remaining cheese. Top each slice with another piece of bread and press to secure.

4   Working in batches, soak each "toast" in the egg mixture for about 1 minute; flip and soak the other side.

5   While the toasts are soaking, coat a large sauté pan with olive oil and bring the pan to medium heat. Working in batches so you don't crowd the pan, cook the toasts for 2 to 3 minutes per side. The toasts should be golden brown, lovely, and crisp—YUM! Transfer the toasts to a baking sheet and place in the oven to keep warm.

FOR THE FRIED EGGS AND ASSEMBLY

1   Coat a large nonstick sauté pan lightly with olive oil and bring to medium heat. Add the eggs to the pan, working in batches if necessary. Cook them until the whites are cooked through and the yolks are warm and runny, 3 to 4 minutes.

2   Remove the toasts from the oven and top each with a perfectly fried egg. Sprinkle with chives if you like and serve immediately.

i'll toast to that!

own your eggs

I am the egg girl. In my opinion, the egg is the most incredible, edible, versatile, and least respected ingredient in the kitchen. The only other food I can think of that might be almost as versatile as the egg is the potato—but even then, it's really not a fair comparison.

Here's proof: Those tall white hats, the pleated toques classically worn by chefs, are inspired by the egg. There are 101 pleats on each hat, signifying 101 ways to cook an egg. Who knew there could be 101 different ways to cook an egg?

Cooking eggs goes way beyond simple scrambling, poaching, or frying sunny-side up. You can use eggs to make pasta, meringues, and soufflés; to bake cakes, cookies, breads, and custards; to whisk sauces and whip up mayonnaise; and even to glue things together. Egg whites make things light and egg yolks make things rich and creamy. But eggs can be temperamental, so you have to treat them with respect. Sometimes you need to cook them fast so they don't get that sulfurous smell, and sometimes you need to cook them gently so they stay tender and oozy. It all depends on how you're using them.

My feeling about eggs is simple: I love them anywhere, anyhow, anytime. And when I buy eggs I opt for brown ones. And where do brown eggs come from? Brown chickens! Gotcha!

baked eggs
with sausage, mushrooms, and tomato sauce

SERVES 4 TIME ABOUT 1½ HOURS

I "love-plus" the idea of nestling eggs in some savory stuff and tossing them in the oven until they're perfectly cooked—whether it's for breakfast, brunch, lunch, an app, or dinner. You can make the sausage and tomato mixture ahead and then whip the dish together in a snap. These are great for a party—instead of individual ramekins, just put them in one big casserole dish. How easy are baked eggs? HELLOOOOO!?!

MISE EN PLACE

Extra virgin olive oil

1 onion, cut into ¼-inch dice

Kosher salt

Pinch of crushed red pepper

2 cloves garlic, smashed and chopped

1 pound Italian sausage, hot or sweet (your choice), removed from casings

½ pound cremini mushrooms, stemmed and sliced

5 large fresh sage leaves, finely chopped

1 28-ounce can plum tomatoes, passed through a food mill

8 large eggs

¼ cup grated Parmigiano

1 bunch of fresh chives, finely chopped

Big fat finishing oil

ANNE-NOTATION I like to garnish this dish with Italian bread that's been sliced and grilled or toasted, rubbed with a raw garlic clove, and drizzled with big fat finishing oil. Mmmmm!

1   Coat a large sauté pan with olive oil and bring the pan to medium-high heat. Add the onion to the pan and season with salt and crushed red pepper. Cook the onion until soft and very aromatic, 8 to 10 minutes. Add the garlic and cook for another 2 to 3 minutes.

2   Add the sausage to the pan and use a spoon to break it up. Cook the

sausage until well browned, 10 to 12 minutes. Add the mushrooms to the pan, season with a bit more salt, and cook for 2 to 3 minutes; add the sage.

3   Add the tomatoes to the pan. Rinse the tomato can with about ½ cup water and add that water to the pan as well (then recycle the can!). Stir to combine, then taste and season with salt if needed (it will be). Increase the heat to high, bring the sauce to a boil, and reduce to a simmer (BTB, RTS); simmer for 25 to 30 minutes. Remove from the heat and taste to make sure it is delicious. **HINT, HINT:** This part

could have totally been done ahead of time!

4   Preheat the oven to 400°F.

5   Lightly oil the bottom of four 6-inch-wide, shallow ovenproof dishes such as ovenproof cazuelas. Divide the sauce between the dishes and gently place 2 eggs in each dish.

6   Place the dishes on a baking sheet and transfer to the oven. Bake until the egg whites are set but the yolks are still soft and runny, 8 to 10 minutes.

7   Remove the baked eggs from the oven, sprinkle with Parm and chives, and drizzle with big fat finishing oil.

baked eggs-traordinary!

the "french" rolled omelet

SERVES 1 TIME **ABOUT 10 MINUTES**

I did my externship from culinary school at the Peabody Hotel in Orlando, Florida, and every year on Mother's Day and Easter they would have an enormous brunch in the lobby of the hotel. I was assigned to work the omelet station. I had my tall toque, my little burner, and my nonstick pans, and I'd stand there in front of the guests and fill their omelets with loads of ingredients, flip them up in the air, and slide them onto the plate—right in front of them. It was quite a show, and I thought I was really cooking! But on a trip to Paris with my family I discovered the *petit déjeuner*—and the lovely French rolled omelet. It's served rolled around the fillings rather than having fillings baked into the eggs. (I'm a huge fan of goat cheese and fresh herbs, the warm eggs melting the tangy cheese in a cuddly embrace.) This isn't the huge, stuffed breakfast omelet we're used to getting at diners here in the States, but it's a preparation that respects the delicate egg and showers it with grace.

MISE EN PLACE

2 large eggs

Kosher salt

1 teaspoon unsalted butter, clarified is best

ANNE-NOTATION You can fill an omelet with whatever you like. But this is IMPORTANT: Whatever you choose for a filling needs to be cooked ahead of time (e.g., sautéed mushrooms, bacon, blanched asparagus). This omelet cooks so quickly that whatever is rolled inside will not have time to cook on its own, though cheese will melt from the residual heat of the eggs.

1   Whisk the eggs together with 1 tablespoon water and salt until the consistency is very smooth and homogenous—there shouldn't be any lumps of egg whites or you'll have big streaks of egg white in your omelet (it should be perfectly yellow—like sunshine!).

2   Put the butter in an 8-inch nonstick sauté pan and bring to medium-low heat. (Remember, this is a very gentle

(recipe continues)

own your omelet
★ the "french roll" ★

Unlike the American version, this omelet is almost as thin as a crepe—it's light, tender, and fluffy, and is the buttery yellow of the eggs.

Pour the eggs into the pan and gently stir the eggs.

Loosen the eggs from the edges of the pan.

When the eggs are almost cooked, lay in your filling just off center.

Fold one-third of the omelet over the filling and gently press to secure.

Gently shimmy the unfolded side of the omelet onto the plate and flip it!

Voilà!

cooking method and you don't want any browning.) When the bubbles in the butter subside, pour the egg mixture into the pan. Using a small heatproof rubber spatula, stir the eggs and tip the pan around to allow the eggs to fill in any gaps. Swirl the pan around on the burner to loosen the eggs from the sides and bottom of the pan. Then let the eggs sit, to allow them to cook gently from the bottom and set up, about 30 seconds.

3 When the eggs look mostly cooked but still have a sheen to them, turn off the heat. Stand square to the stove and hold the handle of the pan perpendicular to your body. Lay the filling in a vertical line, just off center to the left of the handle. (Unless you're left-handed, then off center to the right!) I know this sounds technical, but it's really quite simple.

4 Using the spatula, fold the left side of the omelet over the filling and give it a little press to secure. Wiggle the pan a little to make sure the omelet has loosened—use your spatula to help nudge it if you need to.

5 Have a serving plate standing by. Slide the right side of the omelet onto the plate and with a quick flip of your wrist, roll the rest of the omelet over the top of it. It should be a perfect rectangle. Again, this may take a little practice, but once you get it down, it's fun!

OHM - let!

carbonara frittata

SERVES 2 TIME ABOUT 20 MINUTES PER FRITTATA

This is a riff on one of my favorite pasta dishes—spaghetti carbonara—which is basically just bacon and eggs with pasta. In this version, I play with the ratio of pasta to eggs. In the traditional dish, the balance is heavier on the pasta and lighter on the eggs. I flip this around and go to the other extreme: more eggs and only a little pasta. Toss the whole shootin' match in a nonstick pan, slide the pan into the oven, and voilà! Carbonara is definitely what's for breakfast!

MISE EN PLACE

1/2 pound pancetta, cut into 1/4-inch dice

6 large eggs, beaten

3/4 cup grated Pecorino cheese

4 twists of freshly ground black pepper

Kosher salt

1/4 pound spaghetti, cooked in salted boiling water for 8 minutes, drained and cooled

1/2 bunch fresh chives, finely chopped, for garnish

1 Preheat the oven to 350°F.

2 Place the pancetta in an 8-inch ovenproof nonstick sauté pan and cook over medium-high heat until the pancetta is brown and crispy, about 8 minutes. Remove the pancetta with a slotted spoon and drain on paper towels.

3 In a medium bowl, combine the eggs, Pecorino, and pepper and whisk until well combined. Taste and season with salt only if needed (the Pecorino is usually pretty salty so be SURE to taste the egg mixture before salting).

4 In the same pan, combine half the browned pancetta, half the cooked spaghetti, and half the egg mixture. Place the pan over medium heat and stir the mixture gently with a heatproof spatula. As the eggs around the edges start to set, pull them in and tip the pan so more eggs run to fill in the gaps. Do this for a couple minutes and then toss the pan in the preheated oven for 5 to 6 minutes or until the eggs are set in the center.

5 Remove the pan from the oven, sprinkle with chives, and serve immediately or at room temperature.

6 Repeat this process with the remaining ingredients for another frittata.

FRITTA- TASTIC!!!!

chilaquiles

SERVES **4 TO 6** TIME **ABOUT 1½ HOURS**

Every culture seems to have its version of the ultimate hangover cure, and in my experience this is the best of what Mexico's culinary tradition has to offer. I first had this dish when I was in the Yucatan for my brother Jim's wedding. Lightly fried tortillas that soften when they're smothered in spicy salsa, topped with eggs and cheese, and usually served with refried beans—now THAT is my idea of a morning-after meal. It didn't exactly make me feel like throwing on my bathing suit, but I did anyway. I chased a big plate of these down with a super-spicy Bloody Mary, headed to the pool for a little nap, and I was right as rain in no time. More recently I found myself in a similar condition after a late night in Chicago, and while there was no pool and the weather wasn't nearly as good, those Chi-town chilaquiles still fixed me right up. And they're great even when I'm not hungover!

MISE EN PLACE

Extra virgin olive oil

1 onion, cut into
¼-inch dice

Kosher salt

4 cloves garlic, smashed
and chopped

1 jalepeño, seeded and
finely diced

2 or 3 links fresh chorizo,
casings removed and
meat crumbled

1 bunch of fresh cilantro,
half the leaves left whole
for garnish and the rest
finely chopped, stems
included

½ 7-ounce can chipotles
in adobo sauce, 1 to
2 chilies finely diced and
all the adobo sauce (add
more chilies if you like it
spicier)

1 28-ounce can plum
tomatoes, passed
through the food mill

Canola oil for frying

10 6-inch corn tortillas,
cut into sixths

1½ cups grated Oaxaca or
Monterey Jack cheese

1½ cups queso fresco,
crumbled

1 cup Mexican crema or
sour cream

6 large eggs

1 lime, cut into wedges,
for garnish

ANNE-NOTATION You can use a bag of tortilla chips here instead of making your own (but I think these fresh ones are much better). Pick your battles!

1 Coat a large saucepan with olive oil. Toss in the onion, season with salt, and bring to medium heat. Cook the onion until soft and very aromatic, 8 to 10 minutes. Toss in the garlic, jalepeño, and chorizo and cook for 3 to 4 minutes more, breaking up the meat with a spoon.

(recipe continues)

2   Add the chopped cilantro, chipotles, adobo sauce, and tomatoes. Season with salt, taste, and season again if needed. Stir in 1 cup water, increase the heat to high, bring to a boil, and reduce to a simmer (BTB, RTS). Simmer for 30 to 35 minutes or until the sauce has a good saucy consistency. Taste and adjust the seasoning if needed.

3   While the sauce cooks, fill a large saucepan with about 3 inches of canola oil. Heat the oil over medium-high heat to about 375°F. (or add a slice of tortilla to the oil—when it sizzles, starts to float, and crisps up, it's ready). While the oil heats up, set up your drying situation next to the stove by putting a couple paper towels on a baking sheet. When the oil is hot, work in batches to fry the tortillas until they are crispy chips. Remove the chips from the oil, drain on the paper towels, and sprinkle with salt.

4   Preheat the oven to 350°F.

5   In a large bowl, toss a third of the chips with a third of the tomato sauce and cheeses. Spread the chip mixture in the bottom of a large ovenproof casserole, top with another third of the chips, sauce, and cheeses. Repeat the process two more times with the remaining ingredients.

6   Transfer the casserole to the oven and bake for 15 minutes or until the cheese is melted. Remove from the oven.

7   When the casserole comes out of the oven, coat a large sauté pan lightly with olive oil. Add the eggs (you will probably have to work in batches to fry all of them—no worries) and bring the pan to medium heat. Cook the eggs until the whites are cooked through and the yolks are warm and runny. Place the fried eggs on top of the chips. Sprinkle the eggs with the cilantro and garnish with the lime wedges. Serve with dollops of the crema.

hola, my little chilaquile!!!

poached eggs

with bratwurst and
cheddar mustard sauce on a pretzel roll

SERVES 4   TIME ABOUT 45 MINUTES

This is a take on eggs Benedict—there's a bread element, a pork element, and a sauce element. You can eat this as an egg dish or put it together as a sandwich. It's meaty, zesty, salty, and cheesy and was inspired by a trip I took to the Midwest. I encountered all these flavors in Wisconsin and they go extremely well on a pretzel roll! If you can't find one, a regular roll or an English muffin works just fine too. This is a dish that just screams, "Eat me!"

MISE EN PLACE

FOR THE SAUCE

2$\frac{1}{2}$ tablespoons unsalted butter

2 tablespoons all-purpose flour

1$\frac{1}{4}$ cups whole milk

Kosher salt

1$\frac{1}{2}$ cups grated extra-sharp Cheddar cheese

3 tablespoons whole-grain mustard

FOR THE EGGS

3 tablespoons white vinegar

8 large eggs

Extra virgin olive oil

4 links bratwurst

4 pretzel rolls, cut in half

FOR THE SAUCE

1   Preheat the oven to 200°F.

2   Melt the butter in a medium sauté pan over medium heat. When the bubbles subside, whisk in the flour. Cook for 4 to 5 minutes or until the mixture reaches the consistency of wet sand.

3   Add the milk and whisk aggressively to combine—bust through any lumps like asteroids! Season with salt. Increase the heat, bring the mixture to a boil, and reduce to a simmer (BTB, RTS). Simmer for 4 to 5 minutes, stirring frequently to prevent scorching.

4   Whisk in the cheese and mustard. Taste the sauce and reseason if needed—at this point it should be really cheesy, zesty, and thick (but if too stiff, add more milk). Remove from the heat and hold in the warm oven.

FOR THE EGGS

1   Fill a medium saucepan two-thirds of the way with water. Add the vinegar and bring to a boil (BTB). Reduce the heat until no bubbles break the surface of the water. The idea is to create an egg Jacuzzi, a very gentle cooking method.

★ ★
(recipe continues) ✶

2   Fill a medium bowl two-thirds of the way with cold water and have it standing by.

3   Gently crack 4 eggs into the poaching liquid and cook for 4 minutes. When they're done, the whites will be cooked through and the yolks will be warm and runny.

4   Remove the eggs from the poaching liquid and transfer them to the bowl of cool water. Repeat this process with the remaining 4 eggs. Keep the poaching liquid handy for rewarming.

TO ASSEMBLE

1   Coat a large sauté pan with olive oil and bring to medium-high heat. Add the brats and brown on all sides, about 10 minutes total. When the brats are well browned and hot all the way through, transfer to a baking sheet and place in the oven to keep warm.

2   Add a bit more olive oil to the pan and place the rolls cut side down. You will have to work in batches. As the rolls toast, transfer them to a baking sheet and place in the oven to stay warm.

3   Bring the poaching liquid back to a warm temperature and gently return the eggs to the pan. This will warm them up without cooking them further.

4   Place 2 halves of each pretzel roll on serving plates. Carefully cut each brat in half lengthwise and then cut each half in half lengthwise to create 4 thin slices out of each sausage. Place 2 slices on each roll half.

5   Using a slotted spoon, remove each poached egg from the poaching liquid and blot on a paper towel. This is a pit stop to prevent the rolls from getting soggy. Place a poached egg on each roll and then top each egg with cheese sauce. Yeah . . . BIG CHEESE!

hot bratwurst - brat - BEST!

fried rice
with sunny-side up egg

SERVES 2 TO 4, DEPENDING ON HOW HUNGRY TIME ABOUT 30 MINUTES

This is Hawaiian hangover food . . . or pretty much anywhere hangover food. When you've been out all night at the karaoke bar and had a few more mai tais than you planned, there is nothing like diving headfirst into a bowl of perfectly fried rice topped with a runny egg and a ton of hot sauce. It's a great way to set yourself straight—and to use up leftover takeout rice.

MISE EN PLACE

Canola oil

1 small onion, thinly sliced

1 medium carrot, julienned

1-inch piece of fresh ginger, grated or finely chopped

2 cloves garlic, smashed and finely chopped

4 scallions, whites and greens, cut on the bias

1/2 pound ham, cut into 1/4-inch dice

1 cup frozen shelled edamame, thawed

1/2 bunch of fresh cilantro, some leaves left whole for garnish and the rest finely chopped

4 cups cooked and cooled white rice

1/4 cup soy sauce

2 tablespoons rice wine vinegar

1 to 2 tablespoons sambal oelek or Asian chili paste (optional)

1 large egg per person

1 Coat a large sauté pan generously with canola oil (it is FRIED rice) and toss in the onion and carrot; bring the pan to medium-high heat. Cook for 6 to 7 minutes, stirring frequently.

2 Stir in the ginger, garlic, and scallion whites and cook for 1 minute more.

3 Toss in the ham, edamame, and chopped cilantro and increase the heat to high.

4 Add the rice to the pan and stir to combine, then let sit and get a little crunchy on the bottom. Toss occasionally, but be sure to give it a chance to get a little crispy, 3 to 4 minutes, and then repeat—resist the urge to stir it too much or it will just get soggy.

5 In a small bowl, combine the soy sauce, rice wine, and sambal, if using and add it to the rice, cooking over high heat, 1 to 2 minutes.

6 Meanwhile, coat a medium nonstick sauté pan lightly with canola oil, add the eggs, and bring to medium heat. Cook the eggs until the whites are cooked through but the yolks are soft and runny, 3 to 4 minutes.

7 Transfer the rice to serving plates and top each with an egg, a sprinkle of the whole cilantro leaves, and scallion greens.

hangover helper!

corned beef hash

with hot cherry peppers

SERVES 4 TIME ABOUT 1 HOUR

When I was growing up, it was always a special treat to have a can of corned beef hash for breakfast. This is the same idea, but much better than whipping out the can opener and serving up a bowl of Mary Kitchen! If you're not a spicy pepper person, use a bell pepper instead, but I like adding pickled cherry peppers to my hash—just thinking about them makes my mouth water. Then toss in some fried onions and potatoes, and you'll have a dish that pretty much scratches any and all brunch itches. Salty, sweet, greasy, and spicy . . . mmmmm!!!

MISE EN PLACE

4 large Yukon gold potatoes, cut into ¼-inch dice

Kosher salt

Extra virgin olive oil

1 onion, cut into ¼-inch dice

1 pound corned beef, cut into ¼-inch dice

8 cherry peppers from a jar, stemmed, seeded, and cut into ¼-inch dice, plus ¼ cup of the juice

½ bunch of fresh Italian parsley, leaves finely chopped

1 Put the diced potatoes in a medium saucepan and fill with water to cover by an inch. Season with salt and TASTE the water—it should taste salty like the ocean. Bring the water to a boil over high heat and cook the potatoes until JUST cooked through, about 8 minutes. Drain the potatoes, spread them out on a baking sheet, and let them cool completely. **HINT, HINT:** All this can TOTALLY be a do-ahead!!!

2 Coat a large sauté pan with olive oil, add the onion, season with salt, and bring to medium heat. Cook the onion until soft and very aromatic, 8 to 10 minutes.

3 Crank up the heat to high, wait 30 seconds, and toss in the potatoes (you may want to add a little more olive oil if the pan seems dry). Cook the potatoes until they start to brown, 5 to 6 minutes—resist the urge to stir, because you want them to get crispy! When the potatoes are nice and brown on the bottom, toss or stir quickly and let them brown again.

4 Stir in the corned beef, peppers, and juice. Taste to make sure it is delicious . . . and YES, it will be spicy. Reseason if needed. Remove from the heat, toss in the parsley, and serve.

that's SOME hash!

homemade ricotta

SERVES **4 TO 6** TIME **ABOUT 30 MINUTES**

Sure, you can buy fresh ricotta, but making it yourself is so easy and the end result is so worth it that I can't imagine why you would. It's almost unfair how big the payoff is compared to the effort—plus I find it's cheaper to make my own than buy a packaged version. All you need is milk, cream, vinegar, and salt—it's super quick and easy (Q&E). Make a batch, serve it warm to your friends while it's still fluffy and delicious, and they'll never leave!

MISE EN PLACE

6 cups whole milk

2 cups heavy cream

1/4 cup white vinegar

Kosher salt

ANNE-NOTATION Before you use cheesecloth it's important to rinse it first to remove any lint—you don't want that in your lovely ricotta!

1   Combine the milk, cream, and vinegar in a large saucepan and season with salt. Gently bring the mixture to a simmer over medium heat. As the mixture warms, curds will begin to form. Continue to simmer for 2 to 3 minutes.

2   Line a mesh strainer with several layers of cheesecloth. Place the strainer over a bowl and let drain for 15 to 20 minutes.

3   Eat the ricotta straight away or store in the fridge.

It's so easy being cheesy!

red bliss home fries

SERVES 4 TO 6   TIME ABOUT 1 HOUR

I LOOOOOVE potatoes. My idea of the perfect breakfast is this: crispy fried potatoes, smoky bacon or sausage, a runny egg (or two!), and toast. If I could eat that every day I would—but for me it's never just about the eggs and bacon, it's the potatoes that are essential. I use Red Bliss for my home fries because they're cute and delicious. If you don't have Red Bliss potatoes you can certainly use another kind, but they might not be quite as blissful!

MISE EN PLACE

2 pounds small Red Bliss potatoes

Kosher salt

3 cloves garlic, 1 whole and 2 smashed

Extra virgin olive oil

1 onion, cut into ¼-inch dice

Pinch of crushed red pepper

2 sprigs of fresh rosemary, leaves finely chopped

1 bunch of fresh chives, finely chopped

1   Put the potatoes in a medium saucepan and fill with water to cover by 1 inch; season with salt and toss in the whole garlic clove. Bring the water to a boil and reduce to a simmer (BTB, RTS). Simmer the potatoes until a fork slides in and out easily, 20 to 25 minutes.

2   Drain the potatoes and let them cool. **HINT, HINT:** The cooking of the potatoes could totally have happened yesterday.

3   Cut each potato into ½-inch chunks.

4   Coat a large sauté pan generously with olive oil, add the onion, season with salt and the crushed red pepper, and bring the pan to medium-high heat. Stir in the rosemary and cook until the onion is soft and very aromatic, 8 to 10 minutes. Toss in the smashed garlic and cook 1 to 2 more minutes.

5   Add the potatoes, stir to coat with oil, and season with salt. Using a spoon or spatula, press the potatoes down onto the pan so a crust starts to form. Let the potatoes brown, 6 to 8 minutes. Scrape the potatoes off the pan and turn them. Repeat this process a couple times. The potatoes are done when they are really brown, a little crispy, and totally delicious. Taste and adjust the seasoning if needed. Sprinkle with chives and serve hot. YUM!!!

i'm in red bliss.

bloody mary
my way

SERVES 4 TIME **ABOUT 5 MINUTES**

There are so many beverages that go well with brunch—fresh-squeezed OJ, coffee, tea, mimosa—there are almost too many choices! That's why I like to keep it simple and just go with a Bloody Mary. But even better than a Bloody Mary at brunch is a Bloody Mary on an airplane! Every time I fly (which these days is a lot) I have two and then promptly fall asleep—it's the perfect way to travel. What I love about the Bloody Marys they make on airplanes is that they keep them pure and simple. They don't take the horseradish thing too far, and they don't add radishes, olives, shrimp, or any other ingredients. Recently I saw a bartender put a piece of salami on a Bloody Mary as a garnish—that seemed ridiculous to me. My Bloody Mary recipe is what you want if you truly want a Bloody Mary and not a mixed salad. It's simple: Use V8 juice instead of plain tomato juice, celery salt (which is key), a bit of sherry vinegar to perk it up, and use a good dose of sambal or sriracha instead of Tabasco for a more complex hit of heat. If I garnish it at all, it's with a traditional piece of celery—nothing else. Mmmmm . . . Mary!

MISE EN PLACE

1 quart V8 juice
    (low-sodium is fine)

2 tablespoons prepared
    horseradish

1 tablespoon Worcestershire
    sauce

1 to 2 teaspoons sambal
    oelek or sriracha (or
    more if you like it spicy)

2 tablespoons sherry
    vinegar

1 tablespoon celery salt
    plus more for rimming

1 lime, cut in half

Ice cubes

8 ounces vodka (or more if
    you like!)

Celery stalks

1   In a large pitcher, combine the V8 juice, horseradish, Worcestershire, sambal, vinegar, and celery salt. Mix well to combine.

2   Rim 4 highball glasses with lime juice and then dip them in a bowl of celery salt to coat. Fill the glasses three-quarters of the way with ice cubes. Add 2 ounces vodka per glass and fill with the Bloody Mary mixture.

3   Garnish with celery and serve.

that's bloody delicious!

my perfect fruit smoothie

SERVES 1 TIME **ABOUT 5 MINUTES**

The key to a good fruit smoothie is to keep it from getting watery. If you use frozen fruit, you don't need to add ice and your smoothie will stay thick and flavorful. My favorite combo is mango, pineapple, banana, and strawberry. So I prep the mango, pineapple, and strawberries ahead of time and freeze them (you want the banana fresh so it stays creamy) and then use fresh OJ or apple juice to blend it. If you use just enough juice to get the mixture moving in the blender, you'll have a wonderfully cold, creamy, thick, and luscious fruit smoothie without a hitch. Of course, if you didn't think to freeze your fruit ahead of time you can use a bag of frozen fruit in a pinch—either way it's pretty quick and easy (Q&E).

MISE EN PLACE

1/2 cup 1/2-inch diced pineapple, frozen

1/2 cup 1/2-inch diced mango, frozen

1/2 cup strawberries, topped and quartered, frozen

1/2 banana, peeled and sliced

1 cup orange or apple juice

ANNE ALERT Think to freeze your fruit ahead of time! That's what we call "mise en place," people! You can use any type of fruit you want, pick what's in season, what's at the farmer's market, whatever you like. And don't try this recipe without a blender!

1 Combine the pineapple, mango, strawberries, banana, and juice in a blender. Purée for 2 to 3 minutes, or until very smooth.

2 Pour into a glass. Drink. Enjoy.

Smile.

chef anne sparkler

SERVES 1 TIME **ABOUT 2 MINUTES**

My friend Cesare Casella taught me to drink sparkling wine with ice cubes, and I love it (so much so that now I drink all white wine with ice cubes). Adding ice to sparkling wine makes it like a big-girl soda—and it's my general preference as a beverage. Bubbles make me sparklier! Prosecco is definitely my sparkling wine of choice—it's cheap and cheerful, which is exactly how I like to roll. Pour yourself a big glass of bubbles, toss in some cubes, add a splash of Aperol (a delightful Italian aperitif made from bitter orange and rhubarb—kind of like Campari but not nearly as bitter) and a twist of lemon, and drink up. Mmmmm!!!

MISE EN PLACE	1 ounce Aperol	Lemon twist
Ice cubes	5 ounces Prosecco	

1 Fill a large white wine glass about halfway with ice cubes.

2 Add the Aperol to the wine glass, then the Prosecco. Top with a twist.

this makes me feel so sparkly!!!

Steak Sandwich with Onions, Camembert, Fried Egg, and Chimichurri

sandwiches

I'm like Joey from *Friends*—my favorite

food is sandwiches. To me, it isn't just about slapping something between two slices of bread and calling it lunch. There's an art to making a sandwich. The ultimate sandwich requires the appropriate bread, the proper filling, the perfect *ratio* of bread to filling, some sort of spread to hold the whole thing together, and most important, every bite of a sandwich needs to taste exactly the same.

Consider the sandwich: What's in it? Start with the main ingredient. If you're using turkey, ham, salami, or any other meat, it needs to be sliced thin and crinkled in lovely layers, not just one fat steak of lunchmeat plunked on a roll. Then you need to choose a kind of bread that suits the filling. (If you have a big, hearty, meat-filled sandwich, you want a hearty roll or something thick that can stand up to it as an equal counterpart.) The ratio of bread to filling needs to be just right, and every bite should include a little bit of every ingredient so all flavors come together to achieve the same mission—deliciousness! All the flavors, textures, and even the temperature have to work together! It's imperative that they live with one another in harmony—and they each deserve respect. A great sandwich can be a mind-blowing experience. And the possibilities are endless. THE ONLY THING THAT LIMITS A SANDWICH IS YOUR OWN CREATIVITY.

Often I am asked what my last meal would be. I always say that it would be a PERFECT BLT: delicately toasted bread, crisp but still pliable with a gossamer coating of mayo on both sides, topped with summer's best tomatoes just kissed by the sun—not too thick and not too thin. The tomatoes would be sprinkled with salt so they give up their lovely juices, and then topped with beautifully fried bacon so it's not limp but not too crispy either. It would have a layer of freezing-cold iceberg lettuce right there in the middle for a crunchy burst of juiciness. (People knock iceberg, but it's the perfect sandwich lettuce—crispy and crunchy. It may not be my go-to for salads, but for sammies, it's essential.) Sitting at a picnic table under starry skies, surrounded by my favorite people, enjoying lots of laugher, a pitcher of cold beer, and THIS BLT . . . THAT is my idea of a perfect sandwich.

focaccia

SERVES **4 TO 6** TIME **ABOUT 3 HOURS**

The traditional Italian bread is actually one of the easiest leavened breads to make. Even if making bread scares you (yes, it takes a bit of time), this one is a super cinch to whip together and great for lots of things—it's a multitasking bread. No wonder I love it! Use the focaccia for sandwiches, serve with dips, or just eat it!

MISE EN PLACE

1³/₄ cups WARM—not hot, not cool—water

1 ¹/₄-ounce package active dry yeast

1 tablespoon sugar

5 cups all-purpose flour, plus more for kneading

1 tablespoon kosher salt

1 cup extra virgin olive oil, plus more as needed for the mixing bowl

Coarse sea salt

1 Combine the warm water, yeast, and sugar in a small bowl and let sit in a warm place for about 15 minutes or until the mixture is bubbly and aromatic. NOTE: It's really important that this whole setup be WARM—if it's too hot the yeast will die, and if it's too cool the yeast won't activate.

2 In the bowl of a stand mixer, combine the flour, kosher salt, ¹/₂ cup of the olive oil, and the yeast mixture. Using the dough hook attachment, work the mixture on medium speed until the dough comes together. Continue to knead the dough for 6 to 7 minutes or until it's really smooth and supple. If the dough is too tacky, add a sprinkey-dink of flour.

3 Sprinkle a clean work surface liberally with flour. Turn the dough out and knead it by hand 3 or 4 times. Coat the inside of the mixer bowl lightly with a few drops of olive oil. Return

the dough to the bowl, cover with plastic wrap or a tea towel, and let it hang out in a warm place for 1 hour or until the dough has doubled in size. NOTE: A warm place is key to allowing the yeast to work its magic.

4 Coat a jelly roll pan with the remaining ¹/₂ cup olive oil (this may seem excessive but focaccia IS an oily, crusty bread—that's why it's SOOOOO delicious). Turn the dough out onto the pan and squish it out evenly to fit the size. Turn over the dough to coat the other side with olive oil. Continue to spread the dough out to fit the pan. As you do this, spread out your fingers and use them to poke holes all the way through the dough—it's fun!!! Yes, I know it may seem strange, but as the dough rises again it will create the characteristic "craggy" look that

(recipe continues)

own your focaccia

★ THE CLASSIC ITALIAN BREAD WITH DIMPLES ★

The key to making focaccia is tons and tons of olive oil. . . accept it and move on!

Combine all the ingredients and knead.

Let the dough rise in an oiled mixing bowl.

Transfer to a well-oiled jellyroll pan.

Squish the dough out to fit the size of the pan in an even layer.

Spread your fingers apart to actually make holes in the dough—this will create the classic craggy focaccia.

Let the dough rise again, sprinkle with sea salt, and bake.

makes focaccia unique. Sprinkle the top of the focaccia with the coarse sea salt. Place the pan in a warm (yes, again with the warm) place and let the dough rise for 1 hour.

5   While the dough finishes rising, preheat the oven to 425°F.

6   Bake the focaccia for 20 to 25 minutes or until the top and bottom are golden brown. Remove the focaccia from the oven and let cool completely before cutting.

focaccia goodness ...

lamb meatballs
with tzatziki

SERVES 4 TIME ABOUT 1½ HOURS, ABOUT 1 HOUR UNATTENDED

I'm a huge fan of any kind of meatball. Call it a meatball and I'll eat it. But show me a lamb meatball with some garlic thrown in and a zesty yogurt-dill dipper (a.k.a. tzatziki—a Greek dip that is the perfect accoutrement for these yummy little lamb meatballs), and I'm a happy, happy girl. These flavors were just made for each other! I'll hoover those bad boys like it's nobody's business, and now you can too!

MISE EN PLACE

FOR THE TZATZIKI

½ English cucumber, coarsely grated

1 cup plain Greek yogurt

2 cloves garlic, smashed and finely chopped

1 tablespoon white vinegar

1 bunch of fresh dill, finely chopped

½ bunch of fresh mint, leaves finely chopped

Kosher salt

FOR THE MEATBALLS

Extra virgin olive oil

1 small red onion, cut into ¼-inch dice

Kosher salt

Pinch of crushed red pepper

2 cloves garlic, smashed and finely chopped

1½ pounds ground lamb

½ bunch of fresh mint, leaves cut into a chiffonade

½ cup bread crumbs

½ cup chicken stock

½ recipe Homemade Pita Bread (page 59) or store-bought pita bread

1½ cups washed baby arugula

1 small red onion, thinly sliced

1 cup crumbled feta cheese

FOR THE TZATZIKI

1   In a small bowl, combine the cucumber, yogurt, garlic, vinegar, dill, and mint. Season with salt. Taste to make sure it's delicious and reseason if needed. Let sit for 1 hour at room temp to let the flavors really come together. (If you're making this ahead of time, be sure to store it in the fridge.)

FOR THE MEATBALLS

1   Preheat the oven to 300°F.

2   Coat a large sauté pan with olive oil and add the onion. Season with salt and crushed red pepper and bring the pan to medium-high heat. Cook the onion for 5 to 6 minutes or until soft and very aromatic. Add the garlic and cook for 1 to 2 minutes. Remove from the heat, transfer to a small bowl, and

(recipe continues)

SANDWICHES   177

let cool. But SAVE THE PAN—don't wash it. Look at me, saving you time and dishes.

3 In a large bowl, combine the lamb, mint, bread crumbs, cooled onion mixture, and ½ cup water. Season the mixture with salt and squish with your hands to combine well. Make a small "tester patty," cook it, and eat it to make sure the mix is seasoned properly. Reseason if needed. Then roll the mixture into 12 equal balls.

4 Wipe out the onion pan with a paper towel (if you didn't remember to save it, don't sweat it), coat it generously with fresh olive oil, and bring it to medium-high heat. Add the meatballs and brown them really well on all sides—BROWN FOOD TASTES GOOD!

5 When the meatballs are all REALLY well browned, add the chicken stock, cover the pan, and cook for 3 to 4 minutes. Remove the lid, swirl the pan around a little to kinda glaze the balls, and cook until the stock has evaporated, another 2 to 3 minutes.

6 While the meatballs are cooking, wrap the pita breads in foil and place in the oven for 10 minutes.

7 To assemble the sandwiches, cut each pita bread in half. Place 3 meatballs in a row in the center of each pita, add the arugula and onions, drizzle with the tzatziki sauce, and sprinkle with feta.

annie had a lamb ... meatball!

killer turkey burgers

SERVES 4 TIME **ABOUT 45 MINUTES**

Unfortunately, I've eaten a lot of dry turkey burgers in my day. But I'm on a mission to right all that's wrong in turkeyburgerdom. This recipe was invented out of pure necessity when I was visiting my sister. I had just gotten off a plane and dropped my bags at her house when she said, "We're having turkey burgers for dinner . . . can you make them?" I looked in her pantry and just grabbed some stuff. She had a can of water chestnuts hanging out in there so I decided to put a crunchy little twist on dinner. I added some soy, sautéed onion, ginger, garlic, and cilantro to the mix, and voilà! The killer turkey burger was born.

MISE EN PLACE

Extra virgin olive oil

1 onion, cut into
¼-inch dice

Kosher salt

2 cloves garlic, smashed
and finely chopped

1½ pounds ground turkey

1-inch piece of fresh ginger,
peeled and grated

1 8-ounce can water
chestnuts, coarsely
chopped (not too fine—
they add GREAT texture)

¼ cup soy sauce

2 tablespoons sambal
oelek or Asian chili
paste (optional, but
recommended)

½ bunch of fresh cilantro,
leaves finely chopped

4 burger buns (I like the
seeded ones)

GARNISHES (ALL OPTIONAL, GARNISH HOWEVER YOU LIKE)

4 slices American or
Cheddar cheese
(American melts better)

4 slices beefsteak tomatoes

4 slices red onion

4 leaves butter lettuce

½ cup mayo mixed with
2 teaspoons sambal oelek

1   Coat a large sauté pan with olive oil and toss in the onion. Season with salt and bring the pan to medium heat. Cook the onion until soft and very aromatic, 7 to 8 minutes. Add the garlic and cook for another 1 to 2 minutes. Turn off the heat and let cool.

2   In a large mixing bowl, combine the turkey, ginger, water chestnuts, soy sauce, sambal, cilantro, and the cooked onions and garlic. (NOTE: Save the onion pan to cook the burgers in later!) Add ¼ to ½ cup water to the mix—this will keep the burgers really moist! Use your hands to squish the mixture until everything is really well combined.

3   Make, cook, and eat a little tester patty to be sure the turkey is really delicious. If the seasoning isn't just right, add a little more soy or a sprinkey-dink of salt. When you're confident the burger mix is perfectly seasoned, form it into 4 equal patties.

4   With a paper towel, wipe out the sauté pan you used to cook the onion, coat the pan with fresh olive oil, and bring it to medium-high heat. Add the burgers, being sure not to crowd the pan—if you need to work in batches, knock yourself out. Cook the burgers for 5 to 6 minutes on each side. The burgers should be browned and cooked through when done. If working in batches, keep the first batch warm in a 200°F. oven while cooking the second batch.

5   Toast the burger buns, top with the burgers, and garnish as desired.

these burgers are a real turkey!

cubano toscano

SERVES 4 TIME ABOUT 4 HOURS, LARGELY UNATTENDED

This is my version of a Cuban sandwich inspired by the flavors of Tuscany. Finocchiona (fennel salami), Fontina cheese, fennel-braised pork shoulder, and pickled fennel are the key ingredients in this little lovely—and they are all cousins to those traditionally used in a Cubano. I realize this isn't a twenty-minute toss-it-together-and-eat-it deal. But when you plan ahead and make the commitment to this sandwich it's totally worth it.

MISE EN PLACE

1 pound pork shoulder or butt, cut in half

1 tablespoon fennel seed, toasted and finely ground

Kosher salt

Extra virgin olive oil

1 Spanish onion, cut lengthwise into ½-inch slices

Pinch of crushed red pepper

½ cup dry white wine

2 cups chicken stock

¾ cup red wine vinegar

2 teaspoons sugar

1 fennel bulb, thinly sliced on a mandoline

4 ciabatta sandwich rolls

½ cup Dijon mustard

½ pound finocchiona (fennel salami), thinly sliced

½ pound Fontina cheese, sliced

ANNE ALERT This is definitely a recipe to plan ahead, but you'll be glad you did.

Preheat the oven to 400°F.

2   Dust the pork shoulder with the ground fennel and season generously with salt. Coat a large, straight-sided ovenproof sauté pan with olive oil and bring the pan to high heat. Add the pork shoulder and brown it really well on all sides, about 8 minutes per side. Lower the heat if needed.

3   Remove the pork from the pan and reserve. Ditch the fat and add fresh oil. Toss the onion in the pan and season with salt and crushed red pepper. Cook the onion over medium heat until really soft and aromatic, 7 to 8 minutes. Add the white wine and cook until reduced by about half.

4   Return the pork to the pan, add the chicken stock, and bring to a boil. Cover the pan with foil and toss the whole thing in the oven. Cook the pork for 2 hours, turning after the first hour. **HINT, HINT:** This can be done ahead!

5   While the pork is in the oven, in a small bowl, combine the red wine vinegar with ½ cup water, 2 teaspoons salt, and the sugar. Toss in the fennel slices and let sit for at least 1 hour.

(recipe continues)

6   Remove the foil and let the pork cook for another 20 minutes or until the liquid has almost completely evaporated. Remove from the oven. When cool enough to handle, pull or shred the pork and then combine with the onions in the bottom of the pan. Reserve.

7   Reduce the oven temperature to 350°F.

8   Slice each ciabatta roll in half lengthwise, leaving one long side intact, and open like a book. Scoop out the bready inside of the roll and ditch it. Spread a thin layer of Dijon evenly on both sides and be sure to cover every bit—don't miss any corners!

9   Spread an even layer of the braised pork on the bottom half of the roll. Place 2 or 3 slices of the pickled fennel in an even layer on top of the pork. Lay 2 or 3 slices of finocchiona on top of the fennel, then 2 slices of Fontina, and close the rolls, pressing to secure.

10 Wrap each sandwich in foil and press hard to really secure. Bake the sandwiches until they are hot all the way through and the cheese is melty, about 20 minutes.

It's a SUPER tuscan!!

soprasetta and mortadella sandwich

with pickled hot peppers

SERVES 4 TIME ABOUT 2 HOURS, MOSTLY UNATTENDED

This takes me back to Italy when I was a student on an EXTREMELY tight budget. I was so poor I would go out and wander past all the pretty restaurants I couldn't afford to eat in and think, "Someday!!!" Then I would go buy some bread, cheese, and salumi and make a sandwich to eat in the park. Every time though, I'd think, "This sandwich is SOOOOO good, this is exactly what I WANT to be eating!" I was such a happy girl—just me and my sammie. I didn't feel like I was missing out on anything after all. Sometimes to this day, just for fun, I eat a sandwich in a park.

MISE EN PLACE

FOR THE PICKLED HOT PEPPERS

1/2 pound Fresno peppers

2 red bell peppers

3 cloves garlic, thinly sliced

1/2 cup red wine vinegar

1 tablespoon kosher salt

1 tablespoon sugar

FOR THE SANDWICHES

4 ciabatta sandwich rolls

1/2 cup red wine vinegar

1/2 cup extra virgin olive oil

1/2 pound Provolone cheese, sliced

1/2 pound mortadella, thinly sliced

1/2 pound sweet soprasetta, thinly sliced

FOR THE PICKLED HOT PEPPERS

1 Preheat the grill or broiler.

2 Grill the Fresno and bell peppers until they are BLACK on all sides, 4 to 6 minutes. Put the peppers in a large bowl, cover with plastic wrap, and let hang out for 15 minutes. Remove the plastic and let cool.

3 Using your fingers, scrape off all of the black, charred skin from the peppers. Remove the stems and seeds and coarsely chop the peppers.

4 In a small bowl, combine the peppers, sliced garlic, vinegar, salt, and sugar. Let the mixture sit at room temp for at least 1 hour. (You can also make a big batch and store it indefinitely in the fridge!)

(recipe continues)

TO ASSEMBLE THE SANDWICHES

1   Preheat the oven to 350°F.

2   Cut the ciabatta lengthwise in half, leaving one long side intact. Open the bread like a book, scoop out the bready filling, and discard.

3   In a small bowl, combine the vinegar and olive oil. Brush the insides of the rolls evenly with the vinaigrette—don't miss any corners!!!

4   Lay 2 pieces of Provolone on half of each roll. Spread an EVEN layer of pickled peppers over the Provolone— so EVERY bite will be the same!

Crinkle (crinkle, not fold) 2 pieces of mortadella and lay them gently in a fluffy, even layer over the peppers for a great bite. Then lay 2 pieces of the soprasetta over the mortadella. Be SURE that everything is evenly distributed throughout the sandwich. Close the rolls and give a little press to secure everything. Wrap each sandwich in foil and press once more to really flatten them.

5   Bake the sammies for 15 to 20 minutes, or until the cheese is melted and they are hot all the way through.

BIG MEAT... sandwich!!

sicilian tuna,
caponata, provolone, and arugula panino

SERVES 4 TIME ABOUT 15 MINUTES WITH PREVIOUSLY MADE CAPONATA

Being a cohost on *Worst Cooks in America,* I've seen people do a lot of terrible things with a can of tuna fish. This is not one of them! Sicilian tuna comes packed in olive oil, and it's pricey compared to regular tuna, but it's delicious and worth it. I used to get this sandwich at a shop on Sullivan Street in SoHo when I worked over there. It was called Melampo, run by an old Italian guy who told you exactly where to stand or you'd get yelled at and be in danger of not getting your sandwich. He may have been cranky, but his sandwiches were so good, I never risked pissing him off. Seeded semolina bread, super-tangy caponata, sharp Provolone, spicy arugula—this panino was delightful, even if he wasn't.

MISE EN PLACE
4 semolina sandwich rolls
   with sesame seeds

2 cups or ½ recipe
   Caponata (page 222), at
   room temp

2 cans Sicilian tuna packed
   in olive oil, drained

8 slices sharp Provolone
   cheese

2 cups baby arugula

1   Split the rolls lengthwise, leaving one long side intact, and open like a book. Scoop out the bready inside of the rolls and ditch it.

2   Spread about ½ cup of caponata evenly on the bottom half of each roll.

3   Spread an even layer of tuna over the caponata.

4   For each sandwich, place 2 pieces of Provolone over the tuna and spread an even layer of arugula over the Provolone.

5   Close the sandwich and press to secure it shut. Cut it in half and serve.

My favorite sandwich EVER!!!

taleggio grilled cheese
with bacon and honey crisp apples

SERVES 4 TIME ABOUT 40 MINUTES

Who doesn't love a grilled cheese sandwich? I've eaten a ton of them in my life, and I still love them. But now everywhere I go restaurants feature "comfort food," trying to re-create the familiar grilled cheese on white bread we all grew up eating with canned tomato soup. Been there, done that (BTDT)! So I came up with this upscale grilled cheese: stinky Taleggio, crisp apples, smoky bacon, spicy Dijon, and some crunchy bread sliced not too thick, but fat with flavor. THAT, my friends, is comfort food.

MISE EN PLACE

1¼ pounds Taleggio cheese

12 slices bacon

8 slices rye bread

8 tablespoons (1 stick) unsalted butter, at room temp

½ cup Dijon mustard

1 Honey Crisp apple, peeled and sliced really thin on a mandoline

1   Toss the Taleggio in the freezer for 20 minutes to get it really nice and firm (don't forget about it!). Remove the orange rind and cut the cheese into slices about ¼ inch thick.

2   While the cheese is in the freezer, cook the bacon in a large sauté pan over medium heat until brown and crispy on both sides. When the bacon is done, transfer it to a plate lined with paper towels and reserve.

3   Spread each piece of bread with a thin, even layer of butter. Spread the OTHER side of each piece of bread with Dijon. Lay the bread down on a baking sheet with the Dijon side facing up. YES, I know it will be a little messy. Accept it and move on. This is the reality of grilled cheese. The mess is worth it!

4   Place an even layer of Taleggio on each piece of bread. Lay 3 bacon slices each on 4 pieces of the Taleggio-lined bread. Top the bacon with an even layer of apple slices (these are the bottoms, the ones with just cheese are the tops—together they make a pair!).

5   Preheat a griddle or nonstick sauté pan to medium. You will most likely have to work in batches, so also preheat the oven to 200°F. to keep the finished sandwiches warm. Place pairs of tops and bottoms (not yet sandwiched together) on the griddle or in the nonstick pan and cook until the buttered side gets brown and crusty and the cheese begins to melt, 5 to 7 minutes. When the cheese is nice and melty, flip the top onto the bottom so the cheese is on the

inside. Give each sandwich a press, flip it over, and cook for 1 to 2 minutes more. Keep the finished sandwiches in the oven and repeat the process with the remaining tops and bottoms.

6   Cut the sandwiches in half on the bias and serve hot.

stinky, cheesy delightfulness...

leftover thanksgiving dinner sandwich

SERVES **4** TIME **ABOUT 15 MINUTES**

This sandwich is the reason I make sure to get an extra big turkey at Thanksgiving. I make enough so that even after I send people home with doggie bags, I still have leftovers for me. It's a reprise of my perfectly composed Thanksgiving bite: turkey, stuffing, gravy, and mashed potatoes. I use the gravy as the mayo, add a lovely layer of turkey, some stuffing and mash, and serve it all on toast. THIS to me is the perfect finish to T-giving. Dinner is only half the holiday.

MISE EN PLACE

8 slices sourdough bread

Leftover gravy (page 85)

Leftover mashed potatoes

Leftover stuffing (page 214)

Leftover turkey, sliced (page 83)

Kosher salt

Leftover cranberry sauce (page 225; optional, I opt not)

ANNE-NOTATION The key to this sandwich is even and thin layers of everything. AND, with the exception of the bread, it's totally made up of leftovers.

1   Toast the bread. If you like your sandwich warm, preheat the oven to 375°F.

2   While the toast is still hot, spread each slice evenly with cold gravy (this acts like mayo to hold the whole shootin' match together in a delicious hug).

3   Spread the top piece of bread with a thin, even layer of cold mashed potatoes. Spread the bottom piece of bread with an even layer of cold stuffing.

4   Top each layer of stuffing with an even layer of turkey. Give the turkey a little sprinkey-dink of salt. Spread the turkey lightly yet evenly with cranberry sauce if using (I don't). Place the top piece of bread on the sandwich and press to secure.

5   If you are a "coldie" like me, cut the sandwich in half on the bias and dig in. If you are a "warmie," toss the sandwich in the oven for 10 minutes or until it's warmed through. Flip it over halfway through the cooking time so the bottom bread doesn't get soggy and the top half doesn't get too crisp.

leftovers are the new delicious!

steak sandwich

with onions, camembert, fried egg, and chimichurri

SERVES 4 TIME **ABOUT 1½ HOURS**

I love BIG MEAT and I'm a sucker for anything with an egg or cilantro in it. Go and put any of those things between two slices of good bread and I'll eat it. So naturally, when you put them all together—a steak sandwich with egg and chimichurri—that's a combo right in my wheelhouse. Woo-hoo!

MISE EN PLACE

FOR THE CHIMICHURRI

2 bunches of fresh cilantro, finely chopped

½ bunch of fresh Italian parsley, leaves finely chopped

½ bunch of fresh oregano, leaves finely chopped

3 cloves garlic, smashed and finely chopped

½ white onion, finely diced

1 Fresno pepper, stem and seeds removed, finely chopped

⅓ cup extra virgin olive oil

Kosher salt

½ cup white vinegar

FOR THE SANDWICHES

Extra virgin olive oil

1 Spanish onion, cut into ½-inch slices

Kosher salt

Pinch of crushed red pepper

2 10-ounce filets mignons, each cut into 5 or 6 thin rounds

4 Kaiser rolls

½ pound Camembert, cut into 8 slices

4 large eggs

TO MAKE THE CHIMICHURRI

1 In a small bowl, combine the cilantro, parsley, oregano, garlic, onion, Fresno pepper, and olive oil. Season with salt and let sit for 30 minutes.

2 Stir in the vinegar. Just before serving, taste and reseason with salt if needed.

TO MAKE THE SANDWICHES

Coat a large sauté pan with olive oil and toss in the onion. Season with salt and crushed red pepper and bring the pan to medium-high heat. Cook the onion until soft, aromatic, and lightly browned, 12 to 15 minutes. Transfer to a small bowl and reserve. Wipe out the pan with a paper towel, but don't wash it.

3. Preheat the broiler. Season the steak generously with salt and let sit for 10 minutes before cooking.

4. Coat the pan used for the onion with olive oil and place over high heat. You want to get it REALLY hot—the oil should almost be smoking. Working in batches so you don't crowd the pan, cook the steak slices for about 1 minute on each side. Reserve the cooked slices and repeat until all the steak is cooked.

5. Cut the rolls in half and toast under the broiler.

6. Divide the steak evenly among the 4 rolls. Arrange the sautéed onion in an even layer on top of the steak, then drizzle the meat with the chimichurri. Place 2 slices of Camembert on each sandwich and transfer to the broiler for 1 to 2 minutes, or until the cheese is really nice and melty.

7. While the cheese melts, coat a nonstick sauté pan with olive oil and bring to medium heat. Crack the eggs into the pan and fry until the whites are cooked through but the yolks are still runny.

8. Top each sandwich with a sunny-side up egg and finish with a BIG drizzle of the chimichurri. Close the sandwich, squish it, get lots of napkins, and eat the deliciousness.

here's the beef!

ham, gruyère, and focaccia sammies

SERVES 4 TIME **ABOUT 20 MINUTES**

This sandwich always gets my mouth watering: beautiful salty ham sliced super-thin, layered on with lots of love, then goosed up with some briny cornichon relish and spicy Dijon mustard, all squished and bound together with melty, cheesy wonderfulness. THAT'S a great sandwich. It makes me smile just thinking about it.

MISE EN PLACE

1/2 cup cornichons, coarsely chopped

1/4 cup Dijon mustard

1/4 cup mayo

1/2 recipe Focaccia (page 174), cut into 3 x 5-inch rectangles, each rectangle cut in half equatorially through the bready middle (you should have 4 rectangles, each with a top and bottom)

1/2 pound Gruyère cheese, sliced

1/2 pound ham, thinly sliced

ANNE-NOTATION My homemade focaccia is perfect for this, but of course pick your battles. Store-bought is okay.

1   Preheat the broiler.

2   In a small bowl, combine the cornichons, Dijon mustard, and mayo. Spread the inside of each piece of the focaccia with the cornichon mixture. Be sure each piece is evenly coated.

3   Lay 2 pieces of Gruyère on each piece of focaccia. Transfer to a baking sheet and place under the broiler. Cook until the cheese gets really nice and melty, 4 to 5 minutes total.

4   Remove from the broiler and crinkle 2 pieces of ham on the bottom half of each piece of focaccia in a fluffy, even layer. Return the sammies to the broiler for another minute, or until the ham is warm but not crusty.

5   Remove the sammies from the oven, place the tops on the bottoms, and press firmly to secure. Cut in half on the bias and serve hot.

a new level in the ham and cheese department!

SANDWICHES   197

Crispy Crunchy Kale Chips

sides

braised broccoli
with ginger and tomatoes   203

spring veggie stew
with parmigiano   204

mashed rutabaga
with bacon   207

brined potato chips   208

mushy peas   210

stewed chickpeas
with butternut squash and
tomatoes   211

sausage and mushroom
stuffing   214

shaved raw cauliflower
with caper-raisin vinaigrette   216

grilled broccoli rabe   219

crispy crunchy
kale chips   220

yukon gold potato
pancakes   221

caponata   222

cranberry-clementine
chutney   225

I can't tell you how many times I go into

a restaurant, look at the menu, and let the sides determine what I order for dinner. Sometimes I just order a couple of sides and skip the entrée altogether. Maybe it has to do with being a chef and wanting to create my own dish—to put together the pieces of the puzzle that fit best for my own taste. Or maybe it's just because sides, like appetizers, offer so much freedom to get creative—you can mix up so many different ingredients and flavor profiles that you never run out of new ideas and new dishes. There's almost always something seasonal and exciting to try.

The other reason I love sides is that they're low risk—they tend to be less pressure-packed than entrées. They can also make the main event look more delicious than it might on its own. A pork roast is a pork roast, but the sides give it personality. They may require lots of ingredients and rely on multiple cooking techniques, but this is where your creativity comes in and you can really sparkle.

Part of being a good cook is developing your own palate, the way you would develop any muscle. You have to use it, flex it, and learn to trust it. And just like any dish, when it comes to sides you want to think about ingredients, flavor, and even texture. Seasonality also plays a big role in choosing what sides work with what. The simplest seasonal ingredients are the easiest to work with because you have to do the least amount to them. And if you have a greenmarket near you, explore! Ingredients that come into season at the same time often complement each other (think spring lamb and peas or asparagus; pork and autumn veggies). But texture matters too. Keep this in mind: Something crispy and crunchy goes really well with something mushy. They play off each other! Have fun with it.

As a cook, you want to think about all these different contrasts when you choose what sides to pair with what mains. And if you're like me, and just like to whip up a couple delicious side dishes and call that dinner, you still want your menu choices to balance each other and create a lovely and harmonious meal. Super YUM!!!

braised broccoli
with ginger and tomatoes

SERVES 4 TIME ABOUT 45 MINUTES

I'm just crazy for broccoli, but a lot of people don't appreciate this yummy veg beyond the florets—the stems are crispy and crunchy and delicious, and they usually end up in the garbage. Sad! Being able to save something from the trash makes me like them even more. With some spicy ginger, zesty tomatoes, and little coins of broccoli stems added right at the end of the cooking process—you'll have a bowl of broccoli delightfulness.

MISE EN PLACE

Kosher salt

1 head of broccoli, head cut into bite-size florets, stems peeled and cut into 1/4-inch-thick coins (keep florets and coins separate)

Extra virgin olive oil

1/2 onion, cut into 1/4-inch dice

Pinch of crushed red pepper

1 garlic clove, smashed and finely chopped

1-inch piece of fresh ginger, peeled and grated

2 teaspoons coriander seed, toasted and finely ground

2 cups canned San Marzano plum tomatoes, passed through a food mill

1   Bring a large pot of well-salted water to a boil. Prepare a bowl of well-salted ice water. Toss the broccoli florets in the boiling water, swish them around, and let the water come back to a boil. Remove the broccoli from the boiling water and plunge it immediately into the ice water. When the broccoli is completely cooled, remove it from the water and reserve.

2   Coat a medium saucepan with olive oil, toss in the onion, and season with salt and crushed red pepper. Bring the pan to medium heat and cook the onion until soft and very aromatic, 7 to 8 minutes.

3   Add the garlic, ginger, and coriander seed and cook, stirring frequently, for 2 to 3 minutes more.

4   Add the tomatoes and 1/2 cup water and season with salt. Bring the mix to a boil and reduce to a simmer (BTB, RTS). Cook for 10 to 12 minutes. Taste to make sure it's delicious.

5   Toss in the broccoli florets and cook for another 8 to 10 minutes or until the sauce really clings to the broccoli.

6   Add the broccoli coins and cook for 1 to 2 minutes or until just warmed through. Serve hot or at room temperature.

that's bangin' broccoli!

spring veggie stew
with parmigiano

SERVES 4 TO 6 TIME ABOUT 45 MINUTES

This dish is a glorious collection of green lovelies all coming together to create something super delicious—bound by the marriage of butter and Parm. This creamy combination holds the whole shootin' match in a yummy embrace and says, "Hi beautiful spring veg, let us give you a hug!" It's a dish I learned from Lidia Bastianich when I was working at Felidia, and every time I make it, I think of her, my first boss in New York City.

MISE EN PLACE

Kosher salt

1 bunch of asparagus, tough lower stems removed

½ pound sugar snap peas, ends and strings removed

½ pound Red Bliss potatoes, cut into ½-inch dice

Extra virgin olive oil

1 spring onion, julienned

Pinch of crushed red pepper

1 small zucchini, cut into ¼-inch dice

½ cup veggie or chicken stock

½ head escarole, cut into a chiffonade

1 tablespoon unsalted butter

2 tablespoons freshly grated Parmigiano

ANNE-NOTATION Any combo of spring veg will work.

1 Bring a medium pot of well-salted water to a boil. Set up a bowl of well-salted ice water. (TIP: Use the same pot of boiling water and ice water for all the veg—look at us, always thinking!)

2 Dump the asparagus in the pot and let the water return to a boil, 4 to 5 minutes. Remove the asparagus and transfer it immediately to the ice water. When the asparagus is completely cool, remove it from the ice water and reserve. Repeat this process with the sugar snaps.

3 Toss the potatoes in the boiling water, let the water come back to a boil, and cook for 3 to 4 minutes. Remove the potatoes and spread on a baking sheet to cool.

4 Cut the asparagus and sugar snaps into ½-inch lengths. If you're not sure, shorter is better!

5 Coat a large wide pot with olive oil, toss in the onion, and season with salt and crushed red pepper. Bring the pan to medium heat and cook the onion for 3 to 4 minutes or until it starts to soften. Add the zucchini, season with salt, and cook for 2 to 3 minutes.

6   Toss the asparagus, sugar snaps, and potatoes into the pan. Stir to combine and add the stock. Cook until the stock has evaporated by half, 6 to 7 minutes, then stir in the escarole and cook until it wilts, 2 to 3 more minutes.

7   Remove the pan from the heat. Add the butter and cheese and stir the mixture VIGOROUSLY—this should bring the whole dish together. Serve immediately.

i'm spring!

mashed rutabaga
with bacon

SERVES 4 TIME ABOUT 1½ HOURS

It's one of my missions in life to get people to love rutabagas—I'm practically the PR person for the rutabaga! When I was a kid, we were having Thanksgiving at someone's house and I took a "no thank you" helping because I didn't think I would like it. I tasted it and ended up going back for seconds on the sly because I didn't want the other kids to make fun of me for liking rutabaga. Now I love it. Add some bacon, and duh! It's the best ruta-bacon dish ever!

MISE EN PLACE

1 large rutabaga, peeled and cut into 1-inch chunks

½ pound slab bacon, skin removed and saved, cut into ½-inch dice

Kosher salt

3 Yukon gold potatoes, cut into 1-inch chunks

Extra virgin olive oil

¾ cup heavy cream

1   Put the rutabaga and the bacon skin in a large pot and cover with water by about 2 inches. Season the water generously with salt. Bring the water to a boil, reduce to a simmer (BTB, RTS), and cook the rutabaga for 45 minutes. Rutabaga needs to cook for a LOOOOONG time for the natural sweetness to come out. Toss in the potatoes and cook for another 20 minutes, or until the potatoes are fork-tender.

2   While the rutabaga is simmering, put the bacon in a large sauté pan with a splash of olive oil. Bring the pan to medium-low heat and cook until a lot of the fat has melted and the bacon is really lovely and brown and crispy, about 20 minutes. Turn off the heat and set the pan aside. Multitasking—love it!

3   When the rutabaga and potatoes are cooked, discard the bacon skin, and drain and pass the veggies through a food mill.

4   Heat the cream in a small saucepan set over medium heat.

5   Add the bacon and bacon fat to the rutabaga-potato mixture and stir to combine. Add half the cream and whip it all together. Add the remaining cream and whip again until thoroughly combined. Taste and reseason if needed. Serve hot.

that's a hot rutabaga!

brined potato chips

SERVES 2 TO 4 TIME ABOUT 45 MINUTES, NOT INCLUDING OVERNIGHT BRINE

These crispy chips are a labor of love—they take some work, but in my opinion, they're incredibly worth the effort. Accept it and move on! They're the thinnest, crunchiest, most flavorful chip you will ever eat. They're basically the perfect homemade salt and vinegar potato chip—brined in sherry vinegar, they get really dark and really crispy. Serve them with a sandwich—or better yet, put them IN a sandwich. SUPER CRUNCH!

MISE EN PLACE

1 cup sherry vinegar

2 tablespoons kosher salt, plus extra for sprinkling

2 tablespoons sugar

2 large Idaho potatoes, peeled and sliced REALLY thin with a veggie peeler or a mandoline

Peanut or veggie oil for frying

1   To make the brine: In a large container, combine the vinegar, salt, sugar, and 2 cups water. Toss in the potatoes and refrigerate overnight.

2   Fill a wide, deep pot with about 3 inches of oil. Bring it to 350°F. as measured by a deep-fry thermometer.

3   While the oil heats, remove the potatoes from the brine and gently pat them dry to remove any excess liquid.

4   Set up your drying situation: Line a baking sheet with several layers of paper towels and place next to the stove.

5   Working in batches, add the chips to the oil, swish them around occasionally, and let them cook until they are brown and crispy. Be sure not to overcrowd the pan or you'll end up with greasy, limp chips rather than crispy, crunchy ones.

6   When the chips are done, scoop them out with a slotted spoon or skimmer and land them on the paper towel setup. Immediately give them a little sprinkey-dink of salt. Let cool and store in an airtight container (if you can resist eating them all in one go!).

hello my little chippy!

mushy peas

SERVES 4 TIME ABOUT 20 MINUTES

Mushy peas, mushy peas, mushy peas! When the Food Network UK sent me to England for *Secrets of a Restaurant Chef,* the first thing I did after dropping my bags was head to a pub for a pint, fish and chips, and mushy peas. After the long flight, this meal totally restored me—it's amazing what some fried fish and mushy peas will do for you. Enjoy this sweet green purée of pea-ness, I'm good with that!

MISE EN PLACE

3 tablespoons unsalted butter

½ onion, cut into ¼-inch dice

Kosher salt

1 pound frozen peas

1 teaspoon curry powder

3 tablespoons heavy cream

1 Put the butter in a large sauté pan and bring to medium heat. When the butter has melted, toss in the onion, season with salt, and cook until the onion is soft and very aromatic, 6 to 7 minutes.

2 Add the peas to the pan and cook until soft and heated through, 4 to 5 minutes.

3 Add the curry powder and cream, and taste—season with salt if needed. Cook until the cream has reduced by half.

4 Transfer the whole shootin' match to a food processor and pulse, pulse, pulse until the mix is smoothish—you want it to still have a little texture. Taste and reseason if needed. Serve hot.

more peas please!

stewed chickpeas
with butternut squash and tomatoes

SERVES 4 TO 6   TIME ABOUT 2½ HOURS, NOT INCLUDING OVERNIGHT SOAKING

I've said it before, and I'll say it again: I'm a card-carrying chickpea lover. But my mom is a super-lover of butternut squash. So I created this dish for the both of us—it's a great side to anything, but also perfect on its own for lunch with a salad. The warm spices—ginger and cumin—added to the zesty tomatoes, yummy chickpeas, and sweet squash make it an autumnal lovefest of flavors!

MISE EN PLACE

FOR THE CHICKPEAS

1 pound dried chickpeas, soaked overnight and drained

1 onion, halved, hairy end left on

1 carrot

1 celery rib

2 cloves garlic

2 bay leaves

1 thyme bundle

Kosher salt

FOR THE STEW

Extra virgin olive oil

2 onions, cut into ¼-inch dice

Kosher salt

Pinch of crushed red pepper

2 cloves garlic, smashed and finely chopped

3 cups diced butternut squash, cut into chickpea size

2 teaspoons cumin seed, toasted and finely ground

2 teaspoons fennel seed, toasted and finely ground

1 28-ounce can San Marzano tomatoes, passed through a food mill

1 bunch fresh chives, minced, for garnish

ANNE-NOTATION Pick your battles: If you don't want to make chickpeas from scratch, use canned—they work fine too.

FOR THE CHICKPEAS

1   In a large pot, combine the soaked chickpeas, onion, carrot, celery, garlic, bay leaves, and thyme bundle. Fill the pot with water to cover the beans by 2 inches. Bring the water to a boil, reduce to a simmer (BTB, RTS), and cook for about 1 hour. Do the 5-bean test: Bite into 5 beans; if they are all properly cooked, carry on. If not, cook the beans for another 10 to 15 minutes and try again. Remember, beans cook at different rates, so you need to check a few to make sure they're really done!

2   When the beans are cooked, turn off the heat and season the water generously with salt. TASTE the water

(recipe continues)

to be sure it is adequately seasoned. Let the beans sit in the salty water for 15 to 20 minutes to absorb some of the salty flavor. Remove the onion, carrot, celery, garlic, bay leaves, and thyme bundle and discard. Reserve 1 cup of the cooking water, strain the beans, and set aside.

FOR THE STEW

1 BTW, you can start this part while the beans are cooking: Coat a large wide pot with olive oil, toss in the onions, and season with salt and the crushed red pepper. Bring the pan to medium heat and cook until the onions are soft and very aromatic, 8 to 10 minutes. Add the garlic and cook for another 1 to 2 minutes.

2 Toss in the diced squash, cumin, fennel, tomatoes, and the reserved bean water (if you forgot to save the bean water, tap water is fine). Stir to combine, taste, and season with salt if needed. Bring the mixture to a boil and reduce to a simmer (BTB, RTS). Cook for 25 to 30 minutes or until the squash is cooked through. Add another cup of water if the liquid has evaporated too much.

3 Toss in the reserved chickpeas and cook for 15 to 20 minutes or until the mixture is thick and stewlike. Serve hot or at room temp, garnished with chives.

chick peas + butternut squash = SUPER YUM !!

sausage and mushroom stuffing

SERVES **4 TO 6**   TIME **ABOUT 1½ HOURS**

So here it is: My "go-to" Thanksgiving stuffing! It's my favorite and I make it EVERY year. Why? Because I cook Thanksgiving dinner and I really like it! For Thanksgiving, I am adamant about a few things. One is my big, brined turkey, one is this stuffing, and the other is that I need to have a perfectly composed bite every time my fork leaves the plate. Every forkful has to have a bit of turkey, stuffing, mashed potatoes, and gravy—they're all equally important and if one doesn't come to the party in each bite, it's definitely missed. That's just the way I roll on Turkey Day.

MISE EN PLACE

Extra virgin olive oil

4 onions, cut into ¼-inch dice

4 celery ribs, cut into ¼-inch dice

Kosher salt

3 cloves garlic, smashed and finely chopped

1 pound cremini or button mushrooms, stemmed and cut into ¼-inch slices

1½ pounds sweet Italian sausage, casings removed and meat crumbled

2 cups dry white wine

Peasant bread, crusts removed, cut into 1-inch chunks and toasted (about 12 cups)

1 bunch of fresh sage, finely chopped

1 cup walnuts, coarsely chopped

3 to 4 cups chicken stock

ANNE-NOTATION Save time on Thanksgiving and make this stuffing ahead. And take a peek at my Big Brined Herby Turkey (page 83) and Cranberry-Clementine Chutney (page 225) recipes.

1   Coat a large wide pot with olive oil and toss in the onions and celery. Season with salt and bring the pan to medium-high heat. Cook the onions and celery until soft and very aromatic, 8 to 10 minutes. Add the garlic and cook for another 1 to 2 minutes. Add the mushrooms and cook for 3 to 4 minutes.

2   Add the sausage and cook until it's really brown and yummy, 12 to 15 minutes. While the sausage is cooking, break it apart with a metal spoon or spatula—you want the meat in pretty small pieces.

3   Add the white wine and cook until it has evaporated by half. The mix will be pretty soupy—that's okay.

4   Preheat the oven to 375°F.

5   In a large bowl, combine the bread with the sausage mixture. Toss in the

sage and walnuts and pour about half the chicken stock into the bowl. Using your hands, work to combine everything well—really get in there and squish it up, it's fun! Add the remaining stock as needed to create a really moist mix. Taste and season with salt if needed . . . it will be.

6   Transfer the mixture to a large baking dish and cover with foil. Bake for 30 minutes or until the stuffing is hot all the way through. Remove the foil and bake for another 15 minutes to brown the top.

i'm stuffed !!

shaved raw cauliflower
with caper-raisin vinaigrette

SERVES 4 TO 6   TIME ABOUT 2½ HOURS, LARGELY UNATTENDED

Beyond crudités, people don't usually think to serve cauliflower raw. But it truly is my favorite flower—and I love it raw! In this recipe I shave the florets on the mandoline—they look like little cross-sections of brains. They're cute. I toss them in a salty-sweet-acidic vinaigrette and let them just hang out until they become something akin to cauliflower ceviche. It's a little bit of a think-ahead, as you really do want to give the cauliflower time to soften, but it's totally worth the wait.

MISE EN PLACE

½ cup white vinegar

¾ cup golden raisins

½ cup capers

1 clove garlic, smashed

Big fat finishing oil

Kosher salt

1 head cauliflower, shaved into ¼-inch-thick slices on the mandoline (don't worry if the slices break apart, that's the way it rolls)

1 small red onion, julienned

½ bunch of fresh Italian parsley, leaves cut into a chiffonade

ANNE ALERT The cauliflower needs a couple of hours to "cook" in the vinaigrette, so plan ahead.

1   In a food processor, combine the vinegar, ¼ cup of the raisins, the capers, and the garlic. Purée until smooth. While the machine is running, drizzle in ¼ cup of big fat finishing oil. Taste and season with salt if desired (the capers are salty, so TASTE!).

2   In a large bowl, toss the cauliflower with the vinaigrette and combine well. Add the remaining raisins. Cover and let sit for 2 hours, stirring occasionally. This will allow the cauliflower to "cook," or soften, in the vinaigrette.

3   When ready to serve, toss in the onion and parsley. Taste and adjust the seasoning if needed. Serve at room temperature.

this is one delicious raw deal!

grilled broccoli rabe

SERVES 2 TO 4   TIME ABOUT 30 MINUTES

Green veggies aren't something you might typically think about tossing on the grill, but I like to keep things exciting. So go for it! Toss your broccoli rabe on the grill: Its bitter, green, almost mustardy flavor is totally captivating. Add some smoke factor without losing the crunch and it's so lovely, you'll wonder why you never thought of it before. It just belongs on the grill (and then in your belly!).

MISE EN PLACE

1 bunch broccoli rabe, tough lower stems removed

Extra virgin olive oil

Kosher salt

Pinch of crushed red pepper

1   Immerse the rabe in a large bowl of tap water and let it hang out for 10 to 15 minutes.

2   Preheat the grill to medium.

3   Drain the rabe but DO NOT shake off the excess water. Toss the rabe with olive oil and salt and lay it on the grill in an even layer.

4   Cook the rabe for 3 to 4 minutes per side, turning as needed so all sides grill. The rabe should start to soften and char. If it starts to char too quickly, spray or shake a few drops of water on it.

5   When the rabe is tender, remove it from the grill, drizzle with a bit more olive oil, and add a sprinkey-dink of salt and crushed red pepper. Serve hot or at room temp.

rabe & roll baby!

crispy crunchy
kale chips

SERVES **4 TO 6** TIME **ABOUT 45 MINUTES**

I feel like everywhere I go these days people are talking about kale, the superfood. I love kale as much as the next girl, but unfortunately a lot of times the way it's prepared, I find it tastes like diet or health food and I'm chewing it forever. But when you take kale and make it salty and crunchy—I'm sold! It's SO cool how these little green chips bake in the oven with some olive oil, salt, and crushed red pepper. They're almost as satisfying as a potato chip.

MISE EN PLACE

1 large bunch of kale, tough lower stems removed

Extra virgin olive oil

Kosher salt

Pinch of crushed red pepper

1 Preheat the oven to 250°F.

2 Toss the kale with olive oil, salt, and crushed red pepper.

3 Place the kale leaves in a single layer on a baking sheet—use more than one if you need to in order to keep the kale in a single layer.

4 Roast the kale leaves for 30 to 35 minutes or until crispy. Let cool and eat right away or store in an airtight container.

now that's a SUPER food!

yukon gold potato pancakes

SERVES **4 TO 6** TIME **ABOUT 1½ HOURS**

You say potato, I say MORE potatoes!!! I love potatoes—anyway, anywhere, anytime. Take a potato and put something salty and acidic on it and I'm a hooverina. These are my go-to hooverable potato pancakes. Crispy, crunchy, and golden brown on the outside and soft and fluffy on the inside—hello???

MISE EN PLACE

8 large Yukon gold potatoes

2 to 3 tablespoons white wine vinegar

2 cloves garlic, smashed

Kosher salt

2 large eggs

Extra virgin olive oil

ANNE-NOTATION These pancakes go REALLY well with the Balsamic-Braised Beef Brisket (page 86).

1 Grate 5 potatoes on the largest holes of a box grater. Transfer to a mesh strainer and toss with the vinegar. Place a plate and something heavy (like a can of tomatoes) directly on top of the potatoes to help squeeze out any excess water. Let sit for at least 30 minutes. We're looking for really dry potatoes here, folks.

2 Cut the remaining potatoes into 6 to 8 pieces each. Toss the potatoes and the garlic into a large saucepan, add water to cover by an inch, and season with salt. TASTE the water to make sure it is seasoned appropriately. Bring to a boil and reduce to a simmer (BTB, RTS). Cook the potatoes until fork-tender, about 20 minutes. Strain and pass through a food mill.

3 In a large bowl, combine the grated potatoes, mashed potatoes, and eggs. Mix to thoroughly combine; season with salt.

4 Coat a large sauté pan generously with olive oil and bring to medium-high heat. Make a 3-inch tester patty, cook it on both sides until golden brown—about 4 to 5 minutes per side—and taste to make sure the mixture is seasoned perfectly. Reseason if needed.

5 Working in batches, form and cook all the pancakes until brown, crispy, and cooked through. Blot on paper towels, sprinkle with salt, and hold in a warm oven until all the pancakes are done.

now that's my kind of pancake!!

caponata

Caponata is really about summer in Sicily. It's all the beautiful produce of that island tossed together in a bowl of deliciousness. There are about as many recipes for caponata as there are cooks in Sicily, and some versions take a tomato-y direction, while others take a more vinegary route. This is a fabulous combo of both, and while there is a lot of mise en place, once that's done it's easy to whip together. And, it's just as easy to make a big batch as a small batch, and it really gets better as it gets older. So make a big old batch, toss it in the fridge, and dip into it whenever you need a burst of summer flavors. You can put it on crostini, chicken, or a sandwich, serve it with burrata, however you like.

MISE EN PLACE

1 large eggplant, cut into 1-inch chunks

Extra virgin olive oil

Kosher salt

2 onions, cut into ¹/₄-inch dice

Pinch of crushed red pepper

3 celery ribs, cut into ¹/₂-inch dice

1 fennel bulb, cut into ¹/₂-inch dice

6 cloves garlic, thinly sliced

1 red bell pepper, cut into ¹/₂-inch dice

1 yellow bell pepper, cut into ¹/₂-inch dice

2 zucchini, cut into ¹/₂-inch dice

2 tablespoons sugar

¹/₃ cup red wine vinegar

¹/₂ cup tomato paste

¹/₄ cup toasted pine nuts

¹/₄ cup golden raisins

¹/₂ cup large green Sicilian olives, pitted and slivered

2 tablespoons capers

1   Preheat the oven to 400°F.

2   Put the eggplant in a large bowl and toss generously with olive oil and salt. Spread the eggplant in an even layer on a baking sheet, transfer to the oven, and roast until soft and brown, 20 to 25 minutes. Remove from the oven and reserve.

3   Generously coat a large, wide, deep pot with olive oil. Toss in the onions and season with salt and crushed red pepper. Bring the pan to medium-high heat and cook until the onions are soft and very aromatic, 5 to 6 minutes. Add the celery and fennel, season with salt, and cook until soft, 7 to 8 minutes. Toss in the garlic and cook for another 2 to 3 minutes. By now your kitchen should smell really good!

4   Toss in the red and yellow bell peppers and cook for 5 to 6 minutes. Add the zucchini, stir to combine, and cook until the zucchini softens, 7 to 8 more minutes. If the pot seems dry and is starting to burn, reduce the heat and add a few drops of olive oil and about $\frac{1}{2}$ cup water. Toss in the roasted eggplant.

5   In a small bowl, dissolve the sugar in the vinegar and add to the pan. Stir in the tomato paste. Taste and adjust the seasoning if needed. The sugar and vinegar will make things tangy—THAT'S THE KEY to delicious caponata.

6   Toss in the pine nuts, raisins, olives, and capers and cook for another 10 to 12 minutes. Add a little more water if the mixture seems dry, then taste to make sure everything is delicious. Let cool and serve at room temp. Caponata is really good today, better tomorrow—and fabulous the next day!

CAPONATA that's good!!

cranberry-clementine chutney

SERVES 6 TO 8 TIME ABOUT 30 MINUTES

There are differing schools of thought when it comes to cranberry sauce at Thanksgiving. There are the homemade-cranberry-sauce fans and then there are the jelly-from-a-can people. There are the folks who like to slice it and still see the shape of the can, and those who want the chunky bits of fruit and slices of fresh citrus. I think my cranberry recipe will make everyone happy, but it's certainly more for the homemade crew! It's great for scones, for sandwiches, even on toast. And it has clementines in it! They don't call them "cuties" or "darlings" for nothing—they're easy to peel, and taste like candy! YUM.

MISE EN PLACE

1 12-ounce bag cranberries, picked over for stems

6 clementines, zest grated, then peeled, sectioned, and sections halved

1½ cups sugar

1 cinnamon stick

1 star anise

1 cup orange juice

ANNE-NOTATION Be sure to check out my Big Brined Herby Turkey (page 83) and Sausage and Mushroom Stuffing (page 214) recipes too!

1   In a medium saucepan, combine the cranberries, clementine zest and fruit, sugar, cinnamon stick, star anise, and orange juice.

2   Bring the mixture to a boil and reduce to a simmer (BTB, RTS). Cook for 20 to 25 minutes or until all the cranberries have burst and the mixture has thickened. Let cool and serve as desired.

Oh my darling cranberry-clementine!

Churros con Chocolate

desserts

I've said it before and I'll say it again:

I'm more a fan of savory than sweet, but that doesn't mean I don't love to make dessert. I may want only a couple bites of something sweet after a meal, but those final flavors are just as important as the starter or the main, and they need to be respected. That's why all cooks should have some great desserts in their repertoire—so you always leave people with a sweet memory!

My favorite desserts aren't super fussy. I like more rustic, comfy sweets that come to the table and say, "Hi! I may be the final act but I can still steal the show—so eat me!" To make delicious desserts, you will rely on many of the same cooking techniques you use in your savory kitchen, but baking does require more precision. You need to be more exact with your measurements and, in general, don't have as much room for error. But you can still get creative with your flavors. When I bake, I always try to keep things interesting by adding my own "Anne Burrell thumbprint." These tweaks keep dessert creative and exciting.

Learning to bake and make great desserts is important to becoming a better cook overall. And it's fun! Making cookies, whipping up a pie, pulling off a perfect panna cotta—who doesn't want to be able to do that? And you can—because you're the chef of your own kitchen!!!

chocolate chunk oatmeal cookies

MAKES **ABOUT 4 DOZEN** TIME **ABOUT 45 MINUTES**

There's nothing like a good old-fashioned chocolate chip cookie. There's just something so comfy and homey about them. For mine, instead of whipping out the bag of chocolate chips, I buy block chocolate and chop it up to make big chunks of chocolaty goodness. Then I add oats to give these lovelies a nice bite, and finish them with a little sea salt to intensify the flavors. Needless to say, people are always very happy with me when I make a batch of these sweeties.

MISE EN PLACE

2 cups all-purpose flour

1 teaspoon baking powder

1/2 teaspoon kosher salt

1 cup rolled oats

1/2 teaspoon cinnamon

1/2 pound (2 sticks) unsalted butter, at room temp, plus more for greasing

1 cup packed dark or light brown sugar

1/2 cup granulated sugar

1 teaspoon vanilla extract

2 large eggs

12 ounces block dark chocolate, coarsely chopped

1 cup walnuts, coarsely chopped (optional)

Coarse sea salt

1   Preheat the oven to 350°F. Butter a baking sheet.

2   In a small mixing bowl, combine the flour, baking powder, kosher salt, rolled oats, and cinnamon.

3   In a large mixing bowl, combine the butter, brown sugar, and granulated sugar. Using an electric hand mixer, beat together the butter and sugars until light and fluffy, 2 to 3 minutes. Beat in the vanilla. Add the eggs one at a time and beat until well combined.

4   Using a rubber spatula, gradually add the flour mixture into the butter-sugar mixture. Mix until just combined. Fold in the chocolate and walnuts, if using.

5   Spoon tablespoon-size balls of dough onto the baking sheet, leaving about 2 inches between the dough balls. Bake the cookies for 12 to 13 minutes or until just beginning to color.

6   Remove the cookies from the oven and sprinkle each one with a few grains of sea salt—it's really important to do this while the cookies are hot so the salt sticks. Let the cookies cool for a couple minutes, then transfer to a cooling rack. Repeat with the remaining dough.

chunk-a-chunk-a ... super-yummy cookies!

cappuccino panna cotta

with chocolate sauce

SERVES 4 TIME ABOUT 30 MINUTES ACTIVE AND AT LEAST 2 HOURS TO CHILL

Panna cotta is essentially milk-flavored Jell-O. My version tastes like a coffee milk-shake! YUM! It's super cinchy to make but very impressive and a perfect DO-AHEAD. You can make this one day and serve it the next—it's almost unfair how easy it is for the wow factor you get. Dress it up with a little chocolate sauce, and voilà, it's fancy!

MISE EN PLACE

FOR THE PANNA COTTA

4 sheets of gelatin

3 cups heavy cream

³/₄ cup sugar

2 tablespoons instant espresso powder

¹/₂ vanilla bean

¹/₂ cup chocolate-covered espresso beans, for garnish

FOR THE CHOCOLATE SAUCE

4 ounces semisweet chocolate chips

¹/₄ cup heavy cream

2 tablespoons unsalted butter

2 tablespoons light corn syrup

ANNE-NOTATION If you can't find gelatin sheets, you can substitute powdered gelatin, but first you need to "bloom" it in water—which just means dissolving it in a little bit of water until it looks sort of like jelly. It takes only a few minutes. Then you need to dissolve it with your hot liquid—it's easy, but sheets are a lot more fun. To use powdered gelatin in this recipe, first bloom one ¹/₄-ounce envelope in 2 tablespoons water, then add it to the mix, and you're back to business as usual.

FOR THE PANNA COTTA

1   In a small bowl of cool water, submerge the gelatin sheets to soften. They will go from stiff to soft, kind of like the texture of a giant contact lens. Feel one—it's SO cool!

2   In a small saucepan, combine the cream, sugar, and espresso powder. Split the vanilla bean lengthwise down one side, open it up, and scrape out the seeds with a paring knife. Add the seeds and the hull to the pan. Whisk to combine everything.

(recipe continues)

3 Bring the cream mixture to a boil and then immediately turn off the heat. Remove the softened gelatin sheets from the water and squeeze out the excess water. Add the gelatin sheets to the pan and whisk to combine.

4 Immediately ladle the cream mixture into four 6-ounce ramekins and refrigerate for 2 to 3 hours or overnight.

FOR THE CHOCOLATE SAUCE

1 Fill a small saucepan with 1 inch of water and bring it to a boil (BTB).

2 In a medium heatproof bowl, combine the chocolate chips, heavy cream, butter, and corn syrup. Place the bowl on top of the pan of water (this is a double-boiler setup). Reduce the heat to a simmer. Stir until the chocolate has melted and all the ingredients are combined. Remove and use immediately or store in a warm place until ready to use.

TO UNMOLD THE PANNA COTTA

1 Fill a small saucepan with 1 inch of water and bring to a boil, then turn off the heat. Run a paring knife around the outside edge of the panna cotta to loosen it. Set each ramekin in the saucepan for 10 seconds. Place a small serving plate on top of each ramekin and flip it over to unmold the panna cotta. If it doesn't release, put the ramekin in the water for a few seconds more and try again.

2 To serve, ladle a couple tablespoons of the chocolate sauce around the panna cotta and sprinkle with a few chocolate-covered espresso beans.

that's my favorite kind of cappuccino!

almond caramel thumbprints

MAKES: **ABOUT 6 DOZEN** TIME **ABOUT 2 HOURS**

As I've said, my style of cooking is to take classic dishes and put my Anne Burrell thumbprint on them. These cookies *literally* have my thumbprint on them! But clearly, in your kitchen, they will have *your* thumbprint on them. Once you make the cookie, you can fill the center with jam, chocolate, caramel, whatever you want. Create your own thumbprint—it's fun!

MISE EN PLACE

FOR THE COOKIES

1/2 pound (2 sticks) unsalted butter, at room temperature, plus more for greasing the baking sheets

1 cup sugar

2 large egg yolks

1 teaspoon almond extract

2 1/2 cups all-purpose flour

1 teaspoon baking powder

1/2 teaspoon baking soda

Pinch of salt

2 cups sliced almonds, coarsely chopped

FOR THE CARAMEL

1 1/2 cups sugar

Juice of 1 lemon

1 tablespoon light corn syrup

1/4 cup heavy cream

12 tablespoons (1 1/2 sticks) cold unsalted butter, cut into pats

ANNE-NOTATION Flour acts differently depending on a whole bunch of factors—if your dough is a bit crumbly one day, add a few drops of water to pull it together.

FOR THE COOKIES

1 Preheat the oven to 325°F. Lightly butter 2 baking sheets.

2 Place the butter and sugar in the bowl of an electric mixer equipped with the paddle attachment—the one that looks like the peace sign—and beat until creamy and fluffy, 3 to 4 minutes. Add the egg yolks and almond extract and beat for another minute or so, scraping down the sides of the bowl occasionally.

3 In another large bowl, combine the flour, baking powder, baking soda, salt, and chopped almonds. Gradually add the flour mixture to the butter-sugar mixture. When combined, the dough should be soft and homogeneous. Wrap the dough in plastic and refrigerate for at least 30 minutes, until firm.

(recipe continues)

4 When you're ready to bake, take the dough out of the fridge and roll it into $3/4$-inch balls. Place the balls about 1 inch apart on a prepared baking sheet. Using the tip of your thumb, make a hole as deep as you can in each doughball without actually poking through the bottom. Roll your thumb around a little bit to widen the hole—this is your thumbprint!

5 Bake the cookies for 16 to 18 minutes or until they begin to turn golden around the edges. Remove from the oven and cool. While the cookies are cooling, repoke each one with your thumb to create a really nice spot for the caramel. Repeat with the remaining dough.

FOR THE CARAMEL

1 In a medium sauté pan, combine the sugar, lemon juice, corn syrup, and $1/4$ cup water. Bring the pan to medium-high heat. Be careful not to swish the pan around as that can cause the sugar to recrystallize. As the mixture boils, the water will evaporate and the sugar will begin to turn brown, or "caramelize." This is the point when you DO NOT want to take your eyes off it! Things can take a turn for the worse here and there will be no recovery. As the sugar begins to turn gold and move toward golden brown, remove it from the heat and add the heavy cream. As you do this it will bubble up like crazy. Be sure to use a pan large enough to accommodate the bubbling—this stuff is molten and can cause a very severe burn. Whisk the cream until things settle down and the bubbles subside, then add the butter 2 pats at a time, making sure each addition is thoroughly incorporated before adding more.

2 Let the caramel cool slightly, then spoon it into the hole of each cookie and let cool. You'll most likely have leftover caramel sauce, so save it for something yummy—like pouring over vanilla ice cream!

this is a place i LIKE to leave my thumbprint!

apple brown butter crostata

SERVES 6 TO 8   TIME ABOUT 2½ HOURS

I can't remember where I came across this dessert, but it's been with me for years. The brown butter filling is delightful because it works with apples, pears, cherries, berries—whatever fruit is in season and you have on hand. It's flexible that way. But there's more—this sweetie is also really great the next morning for breakfast! YES, there are a lot of steps to this one, but it's all pretty easy and very impressive. Accept it and move on—this will earn you a lot of kudos.

MISE EN PLACE

FOR THE CRUST

1 cup all-purpose flour, plus more as needed

Pinch of salt

12 tablespoons (1½ sticks) cold butter, cut into pea-size pieces

1 egg yolk

¼ cup ice water

FOR THE FILLING

6 tablespoons unsalted butter

½ cup sugar

1 teaspoon vanilla extract

⅓ cup all-purpose flour

1 large egg

FOR THE APPLES

3 tablespoons unsalted butter

6 Granny Smith apples, peeled, cored, and cut into eighths

2 tablespoons sugar

½ cup brandy

½ cup golden raisins

1 large egg beaten with 2 tablespoons water

FOR THE CRUST

1   In a food processor, combine the flour and salt. Pulse once to combine. Add the butter and pulse, pulse, pulse until the mixture looks like grated Parmigiano cheese. Add the egg yolk and half the ice water and pulse, pulse, pulse again until the mixture forms a rough ball. If the mix seems dry, add the remaining ice water and pulse again.

2   Turn the dough out onto a lightly floured work surface. Using the heel of your hand, schmear the dough forward and then roll it back toward you to where it started. Repeat this process 2 more times. DO NOT rotate the dough while you do this—always work in the same direction. If you rotate the dough it will start to get tough, rather than crisp. Form the ball into a disk, wrap in plastic, and

refrigerate for at least 1 hour. **HINT, HINT:** This could have been done yesterday!

FOR THE FILLING

1   In a small saucepan, melt the butter over medium heat and cook until it starts to turn brown and smells like hazelnuts.

2   Transfer the brown butter to a medium mixing bowl, then add the sugar and vanilla, and beat with a hand beater or stand mixer (I use them interchangeably). Gradually beat in the flour. When the flour is combined, beat in the egg. Reserve. (BTW: It's SUPER yummy!)

FOR THE APPLES

1   Toss the butter into a large sauté pan and bring the pan to medium-high heat. When the butter is melted and bubbly, add the apples and sugar and cook for 6 to 7 minutes or until the apples start to soften.

2   Pull the pan off the burner and add the brandy. You want to do this at the front of the pan and then tip it into the flame. BIG FIRE!!! It's fun! If you have an electric stove, this part won't work . . . sorry. Either way, cook the brandy until it reduces and the apple mixture is no longer soupy. Turn off the heat, stir in the raisins, and let the mixture cool.

TO ASSEMBLE

1   Preheat the oven to 350°F.

2   Remove the dough from the fridge and let it come to room temp for 15 minutes before using.

3   Dust a clean work surface with flour and roll the dough into a circle $1/8$ to $1/4$ inch thick. Lay the dough in a 12-inch false-bottom tart pan. There will be lots of dough hanging over the sides—this is what you want.

4   Pour the reserved filling over the dough and spread it out in an even layer.

5   Spoon the apples into the pan on top of the filling and spread them out in an even layer. Fold the dough draped over the sides on top of the apples (you will still see some of the apples and filling—it should look rustic!). Brush the top of the dough with the egg wash and bake for 35 to 40 minutes, or until the top is golden brown and a little bit crispy.

the apple of my pie!!

churros con chocolate

SERVES **4 TO 6**   TIME **ABOUT 45 MINUTES**

What's better than fried dough? Fried dough with chocolate sauce! This is the classic French pâte à choux recipe and it can be used to make SOOOOO many different things—profiteroles, cream puffs, eclairs, you name it. Once you have this down, the whole world of puffy little pastries is open to you. You can dip them in chocolate, stuff them with cream, fry them—any way they puff, these are delicious.

MISE EN PLACE

FOR THE CHURROS

1 cup whole milk

4 tablespoons (½ stick) unsalted butter

Pinch of kosher salt

1 cup all-purpose flour

4 large eggs

Peanut or other neutral-flavored oil for frying

FOR THE CHOCOLATE

8 ounces Mexican chocolate, chopped

½ cup heavy cream

3 tablespoons unsalted butter

2 tablespoons light corn syrup

FOR THE CINNAMON SUGAR

1 cup sugar

2 tablespoons cinnamon

Pinch of kosher salt

ANNE-NOTATION If you don't have Mexican chocolate, you can always substitute bittersweet chocolate mixed with ½ teaspoon cinnamon.

FOR THE CHURROS

1   In a small saucepan, combine the milk, butter, and salt and bring to medium heat. When the butter has melted, add all the flour and whisk to combine—don't worry about the lumps. Switch to a wooden spoon and cook, stirring constantly, until the dough has formed a ball and has a slightly sweaty sheen, 4 to 5 minutes.

2   Transfer the mixture to a medium bowl and let the dough cool for 4 to 5 minutes. Using an electric hand mixer, add 3 of the eggs, one at a time—do not add the next egg until the last one is fully combined. In a small bowl, beat the last egg and add just half of it to the batter, beating the dough and gauging the texture. The dough should be tight, but not super stiff and definitely not loose. If the dough is REALLY tight, beat in the remaining half egg. The dough should be very pliable, but if it's too loose, add a little more flour to get it just right.

3   Transfer the dough to a pastry bag outfitted with a large star tip. Reserve.

FOR THE CHOCOLATE

1 Fill a medium saucepan with an inch of water and bring it to a boil (BTB).

2 In a heatproof mixing bowl, combine the chocolate, heavy cream, butter, and corn syrup. Place the bowl over the saucepan (a double-boiler rig!), reduce to a simmer, and stir occasionally, until the chocolate melts and all the ingredients are combined. Then remove the whole saucepan setup from the heat. Cover the bowl with plastic and reserve.

FOR THE CINNAMON SUGAR

Combine the sugar, cinnamon, and salt in a large, wide, flat dish.

TO COOK THE CHURROS

1 Pour 1½ inches of oil into a large, wide, straight-sided sauté pan and set over medium-high heat. Using a deep-fry thermometer, bring the oil to 350°F.

2 Pipe the dough into the hot oil into sticks or desired shapes. (I like mine kinda curly.) You may have to waste a couple squeezes to get the hang of it, but don't sweat it. Working in batches, fry the dough on both sides, 2 to 3 minutes per side, or until brown and crispy. When the churros are done, transfer them to a baking sheet lined with paper towels for just a few seconds. While they are still really hot, drop them in the cinnamon-sugar mixture and roll them around to coat.

3 Serve the churros hot with a little pot of the warm chocolate sauce for dipping.

arriba!!!

sticky toffee pudding

SERVES 6 TO 8   TIME ABOUT 1½ HOURS

I first tasted this pudding when I went to London (I've never understood why the Brits call all desserts "pudding"). I remember being so full from dinner that I thought I couldn't eat another bite. Then this pudding (it's really cake) came to the table, drizzled with luscious toffee sauce, and I was suddenly hungry again. I LOVED the little pot of toffee sauce that was served next to the pudding—almost more than I liked the cake. The next thing I knew, I looked down at my plate and it was clean! The moral of the story is: There's always room for sticky pudding!

MISE EN PLACE

FOR THE PUDDING

2¼ cups pitted dates

¾ cup dark spiced rum

1 teaspoon vanilla extract

3½ cups all-purpose flour

½ teaspoon cinnamon

Pinch of salt

1 tablespoon baking powder

2 cups packed light or dark brown sugar

8 tablespoons (1 stick) unsalted butter, at room temperature, plus more for the baking dish

3 large eggs

FOR THE TOFFEE SAUCE

1½ pounds (6 sticks) unsalted butter

3 cups packed dark or light brown sugar

1 cup brandy

Whipped cream (optional)

FOR THE CAKE

1 Preheat the oven to 350°F. and butter a 9 x 13-inch baking dish.

2 In a small saucepan, combine the dates, rum, and ¾ cup water. Bring the liquid to a boil, reduce to a simmer (BTB, RTS), and cook for 5 to 7 minutes. Remove the pan from the heat, add the vanilla, and let the liquid cool. Purée the mixture in a food processor until smooth, and reserve.

3 Sift the flour, cinnamon, salt, and baking powder into a medium bowl.

4 Combine the brown sugar and butter in a large mixing bowl and beat until homogeneous. Beat in the eggs one at a time. Gently stir the flour mixture into the butter-sugar in thirds. Stir in the reserved date purée.

5 Transfer the batter to the prepared baking dish and bake for 35 minutes or until set in the middle. Let cool for about 10 minutes.

(recipe continues)

FOR THE TOFFEE SAUCE

While the pudding is baking, combine the butter, brown sugar, brandy, and ½ cup water in a large saucepan. Bring to a boil and reduce to a simmer (BTB, RTS), whisking frequently. Cook over medium heat until the mixture thickens to a sauce consistency, about 15 minutes.

TO FINISH THE PUDDING

1 Using a skewer or chopstick, poke holes in the pudding every inch or so.

2 Pour half the toffee sauce over the cake and let it soak in for at least 20 minutes.

3 Serve the pudding in a warm pool of the remaining sauce. Garnish with whipped cream if desired.

kabocha squash mascarpone cheesecake

SERVES 10 TO 12   TIME ABOUT 3 HOURS

It wasn't until a few years ago that I discovered the kabocha squash. I don't know how I missed it! It's the Japanese version of a pumpkin and I adore it. It's super flavor dense with a lovely texture, and it doesn't have as much water as a butternut squash or a pumpkin, so it's excellent for baking. It's also a pretty deep green on the outside and a happy shade of yellow-orange on the inside—just one more reason to love it. I've even heard that in some cultures the kabocha is considered an aphrodisiac. I'll let you decide whether that's true or not!

MISE EN PLACE

FOR THE FILLING

1/2 medium kabocha squash

Extra virgin olive oil

1 teaspoon cinnamon

1/2 teaspoon allspice

1/2 teaspoon nutmeg

1/2 teaspoon ground ginger

2 cups mascarpone cheese

1/2 cup packed light brown sugar

1 teaspoon vanilla extract

3/4 cup sweetened condensed milk

4 large eggs

2 tablespoons bourbon

FOR THE CRUST

2 cups gingersnap cookie crumbs

1/4 cup packed light brown sugar

1/2 teaspoon cinnamon

Pinch of kosher salt

4 tablespoons (1/2 stick) unsalted butter, melted

Whipped cream, optional

ANNE-NOTATION This cheesecake is best made the day before you plan to serve it.

FOR THE FILLING

1   Preheat the oven to 350°F.

2   Scoop out the seeds and stringy guts from the squash. Cut the squash into thirds and rub each section with olive oil. Place the oiled sections on a baking sheet and transfer to the oven. Bake the squash for 1 hour, rotating the sheet and turning over the squash about halfway through the cooking time. When done, the squash should be fork-tender—a fork should slide in and out easily. Let the squash cool.

(recipe continues)

FOR THE CRUST

While the squash is roasting, prepare the crust: In a large bowl, combine the gingersnap crumbs, brown sugar, cinnamon, salt, and melted butter. Stir well to combine. Press the crust onto the bottom and sides of a 9-inch springform pan. Reserve in the fridge.

TO ASSEMBLE

1   When the squash is cool enough to handle, remove and discard the skin and purée the flesh in the food processor until smooth. Add the cinnamon, allspice, nutmeg, and ginger and pulse to combine.

2   In a large mixing bowl, combine the mascarpone, brown sugar, and vanilla and beat with an electric hand mixer until combined. Beat in the squash mixture along with the condensed milk. Beat in the eggs one at a time until combined, then whisk in the bourbon.

3   Reduce the oven temperature to 300°F. Pour the batter into the prepared crust and bake for about 1 hour and 20 minutes, until set in the middle, rotating the pan halfway through the baking time. If the top of the cheesecake starts to brown, tent it with aluminum foil.

4   Remove the cheesecake from the oven and let cool completely before serving with a dollop of whipped cream if desired. This will be good today—and even better tomorrow.

squash it!

ruby red grapefruit semifreddo

with orange and mango salad

SERVES 6 TO 8   TIME ABOUT 45 MINUTES ACTIVE AND AT LEAST 5 HOURS TO FREEZE

Semifreddo—it's only semifrozen! If you've never done it before, making semi-freddo is a lot like making ice cream without an ice cream maker. I like to think of it as low-tech ice cream—it's super refreshing. You whip the ingredients together, toss it all in a loaf pan, freeze it, slice it, and serve it with some fruit. It really is the perfect (semi!) frozen dessert. And my mom really loves it.

MISE EN PLACE

8 large egg yolks and 1 egg white

1¼ cups plus 2 tablespoons sugar

Kosher salt

1 cup sliced almonds

2 cups COLD heavy cream

Grated zest and juice of 1 Ruby Red grapefruit (about ½ cup juice)

2 oranges, supremed, plus the juice

1 ripe mango, peeled, pitted, and cut into ½-inch dice

½ bunch of fresh mint, leaves cut into a chiffonade

ANNE ALERT This takes some time to freeze, so plan accordingly. Also, you will have leftover sugar-coated almonds, so save them in an airtight container for another use—or just for snacking!

1   Preheat the oven to 350°F. Line a baking sheet with a silicone baking mat or parchment paper.

2   In a small mixing bowl, combine the egg white, the 2 tablespoons sugar, and a pinch of salt. Using an electric hand mixer, beat the egg white until very frothy. Add the almonds and toss to coat.

3   Spread the almonds on the lined baking sheet in an even single layer. Bake for 12 minutes, or until the nuts start to brown. Remove from the oven and let cool for 4 to 5 minutes, then use a spatula to loosen the nuts from the mat. The nuts will be crystallized and very crunchy. Let them cool completely.

4   Line a loaf pan with plastic wrap, being sure to leave plenty of overhang so the plastic can be folded over to cover the top. Sprinkle the candied almonds in an even layer over the bottom of the pan. Reserve.

(recipe continues)

DESSERTS

5 Pour the COLD cream into a large bowl and beat it with the hand mixer until it holds medium peaks. Reserve in the fridge.

6 In a large heatproof bowl, combine the remaining sugar, egg yolks, grapefruit zest and juice, and a pinch of salt. Beat the egg yolk mixture until it's homogeneous and a little bit fluffy, 2 to 3 minutes.

7 Fill a medium saucepan with 1 inch of water and bring to a boil (BTB). Place the bowl with the yolks over the saucepan, reduce the heat to medium, and whisk the mixture constantly until very light and fluffy, 5 to 6 minutes. As an insurance policy, use a candy thermometer to take the temperature of the egg mixture—it should be about 170°F.

8 Remove the bowl from the saucepan and beat the egg mixture with the mixer until it is doubled in size, pale, and extremely light and fluffy, and the bottom of the bowl is cool to the touch.

9 Working in thirds, fold the reserved whipped cream into the egg mixture. Do this quickly but gently. Try not to squish the air out of the whipped cream. When all the cream is combined and the mix is homogeneous, transfer it to the prepared loaf pan and fold the plastic over the top to cover it.

10 Put the pan in the freezer and chill for AT LEAST 4 to 5 hours, overnight, or even for a couple of days.

11 When ready to serve, combine the oranges, their juices, and mango in a medium bowl. Remove the loaf pan from the freezer, open the plastic wrap, and turn the semifreddo out onto a plate. Cut it into 1-inch slices and place on serving plates. Toss the mint with the oranges and mango and garnish the semifreddo slices with the fruit salad. Serve immediately.

only semifrozen – but fully delicious!!

crepes
with mascarpone and chocolate
with cherry compote

SERVES 4   TIME ABOUT 1½ HOURS

Crepes are a blank canvas. You can put anything inside of them—sweet, savory, cheesy, meaty, whatever you want. Once you get the hang of it, they're super fun to make. They may seem fussy and a tiny bit scary at first, but remember, they're just really thin pancakes. The first one or two never work out, but accept it and move on. Once you get the hang of the tilt-a-whirl, you'll get the batter to run around in a smooth, even layer. After that, it's a POC (piece of cake), and you can focus on filling them.

MISE EN PLACE

FOR THE CREPES

2 large eggs

½ cup whole milk, plus more as needed

½ cup club soda

Kosher salt

1 cup all-purpose flour

3 tablespoons unsalted butter, melted, plus 3 tablespoons for cooking the crepes

FOR THE CHERRY COMPOTE

1 pound cherries, pitted and halved

¾ cup sugar

Grated zest and juice of 1 lemon

FOR THE FILLING

2 cups mascarpone cheese

¾ cup chocolate chips or finely chopped chocolate

½ teaspoon cinnamon

¾ cup sugar

Powdered sugar, for dusting

ANNE-NOTATION You want to use a 2-ounce ladle for these crepes. How do you know it's a 2-ounce ladle? It says so on the handle!

TO MAKE THE CREPE BATTER

In a mixing bowl, beat together the eggs and milk. Whisk in the club soda and a pinch of salt. Gradually whisk in the flour and mix until just combined, then whisk in the melted butter. The mix should be the consistency of really thin pancake batter. If it's a little thick, add a little more milk. Let the batter sit for at least 30 minutes before using. **HINT, HINT:** Crepe batter can be made up to a couple days ahead and refrigerated.

★ ★
(recipe continues) ★

TO MAKE THE CHERRY COMPOTE

In a medium saucepan, combine the cherries, sugar, lemon zest and juice, and $1/2$ cup water. Bring the mixture to a boil and reduce to a simmer (BTB, RTS). Cook the cherries until they release their juices and the liquid concentrates and becomes slightly syrupy, about 15 minutes. Remove from the heat and reserve.

TO MAKE THE FILLING

In a medium bowl, combine the mascarpone, chocolate chips, cinnamon, and sugar. Stir to combine and reserve.

TO MAKE THE CREPES

1   In a small nonstick sauté pan, melt $1/2$ tablespoon butter over medium heat. Swirl the butter around to coat the bottom of the pan. Wipe out any excess with a paper towel, saving the paper towel to use again—you will.

2   Slowly ladle $1 1/2$ to 2 ounces of crepe batter into the pan, tipping and rolling the pan around to allow the batter to evenly coat the bottom. It will take a little practice to get the motion of the ocean, the correct temperature of the pan, and the proper amount of batter. Even for an experienced crepe maker, it takes a couple tries to get into the

groove. The first few crepes always get tossed—accept it and move on.

3   When the edges of the crepe begin to pull away from the pan and the bottom begins to brown, turn over the crepe and cook for 1 more minute. Remove the crepe from the pan, let cool, and set aside in a stack separated by layers of parchment paper to keep them from sticking together.

4   Repeat this process with the remaining batter—once you get into the swing of things it's fast and fun!

TO ASSEMBLE

1   Place a couple tablespoons of the mascarpone filling in the middle of each crepe and spread the filling over half the crepe in an even layer. Roll around the filling to seal.

2   Place 2 filled crepes on each serving plate and spoon the warm cherry compote over the top. Dust with powdered sugar and serve.

that's cherry !!!

girl chef glossary

I'm not into fancy culinary terms, but I do have some words and phrases that I use to make cooking easy and fun. This list is just a cheat sheet to help you follow my recipes and not get all bunched up as you rock your stove.

big fat finishing oil This is your big money extra virgin olive oil, the expensive stuff. Heat changes the flavor of olive oil, so this is the oil you want to use when you're after a pristine, green, olive-y flavor to drizzle on pasta, salads, soups, or anything really, just before serving. There are tons of different kinds of olive oil available so experiment with them. You may want to have different big fat finishing oils for different purposes—play around and decide what kind you like best.

brown food What you get when you take the time to sear meat really well and establish big brown flavor and color.

BTB, RTS Bring to Boil, Return to Simmer. In order to reduce to a simmer you must first bring your pot to a boil—you can never turn the heat down if it hasn't gone up!

cinchy Easy.

crud The delicious brown bits on the bottom of the pan that help develop deep, rich, meaty flavors.

equatorially Through the middle widthwise, like the equator!

evaporate To cook liquid until it reduces and thickens. I use these two terms interchangeably.

fork tender When something can easily be pierced with a fork and meets no resistance; how you know it's fully cooked!

girl chef Anne Burrell!!!

homogenous When things are uniformly combined.

lardons Sliced bacon cut crosswise into 1/4-inch lengths.

mise en place French for "put in place." To get all your prep work done BEFORE you start cooking.

POC Piece of Cake, totally easy.

QC Quality Control, tasting to make sure everything is delicious.

Q&E Quick & Easy, the way we like to roll!

reduce To cook liquid until it evaporates and thickens. See "evaporate"!

shootin' match The whole thing, whatever it is.

sprinkey-dink A little sprinkle.

supreme A fancy little way to cut citrus fruit. Start by cutting off all the skin and the outside membranes, then remove each section of fruit by cutting in between the sectional membranes with a paring knife—what you're left with is just the flesh of the citrus without any of the other bits attached.

technique An approach or a method, not a specific recipe (i.e. braising).

index